Return to Creation

A Survival Manual
for Native and Natural People

by
Manitonquat
(Medicine Story)

Bear Tribe Publishing
Spokane, Washington

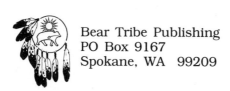 Bear Tribe Publishing
PO Box 9167
Spokane, WA   99209

Copyright© 1991 by Manitonquat

Book Design, Cover, and Illustrations
Copyright© 1991 by George Monacelli

ISBN 0-943404-20-7

Printed on Recycled Paper

Printed and bound by Malloy Lithographing, Inc.,
Ann Arbor, Michigan, United States of America.

First Edition

Acknowledgements

Some selections from this book have appeared in the following periodicals: *Akwesasne Notes, Communities, In Context, Many Smokes, Men, New Age Journal, Star of the East, The Sun,* and *Wildfire.*

I want to thank Wabun Wind for editing and general good advice and encouragement, Michaeleen Kimmey and Marilyn Perkins for editorial support beyond the call of friendship, and Jade Barker, Stephen McFadden, and the men of the native circles in the state prisons at Somers, CT, and Gardner, MA, for reading and commenting helpfully upon the manuscript.

There are so many voices in my head, so many teachers who have bestowed their portion of native wisdom on me, that simple honesty requires that at least a few of the most important be recorded here. Whatever is clear and true in this book derives from their teachings.

A few of those who have left some of their wisdom with me and gone ahead upon the star journey beyond this life are Saupaquant, Senabeh, John Fire Lame Deer, Chief Beeman Logan, Mad Bear, Madas Sapiel, David Monongye, Grace Spotted Eagle, Papasan Eastman, Philip Deer, Godfrey Chips, Don McCloud, Herbert Blake, Chief Red Blanket, and Buffalo Child Albert Lightning.

Some of the many others whose words and lives have been an inspiration to me are Janet McCloud, Thomas Banyacya, Coyote, Tom Porter, Oren Lyons, John Mohawk, Ray Fadden, Rarihokwats, Semu Huarte, Wallace Black Elk, Floyd Westerman, Adolf and Beverly Hungry Wolf, Herbert Blatchford, Phil Lane, Joy Harjo, Leslie Silko, Ilene Depoe Somes, Marcie Rendon, Winona LaDuke, Sun Bear, Wildcat, Big Toe, and Tall Oak.

I acknowledge and thank all the elders, medicine people, clan mothers, chiefs and warriors of the Wampanoag Nation, especially: Massasoit (Supreme Sachem) Elsworth Drifting Goose and Caroline Oakley, Supreme Medicine Man Slow Turtle John Peters and Burne Stanley, Chief Alden Windsong and Bonnie Blake, Evening Star Gertrude Aiken, Dr. Helen Attaquin, Beatrice Gentry, Louise Chumley, Ramona Peters, Russell Peters, gkeesettanamoojk, Lightning Foot Clinton Wixon, John

Sly Fox and Claire Oakley, Wamsutta Frank James, Nanepashemet, Earl Mills, Jr., and Smiling Dove Nancy Eldridge.

I also acknowledge all the contemporary native leaders and warriors who have sacrificed so much, including John Trudell, Dennis Banks, the Means brothers, the Bellacourt brothers, and all those who have been or are now in prison because of crimes committed against their people, especially Leonard Pelletier.

Thanks also to all the non-natives who have devoted so much of their lives to helping secure the legal and human rights of our people. I especially honor my friends Jack Magee and Lew Gurwitz.

Dedication

To My Grandfather,
Wunninam, Good–Bringer

WUNIISH/GO IN BEAUTY

Wuniish, Grandfather.

Wuniish to a world that was not
entirely lost to me while you were alive,
a world that put its face to the sky and smiled,
a world of grace and confidence.
The silent past that grazed
like a doe at dusk on the ghostly meadows
has blinked into the secret wood

Wuniish to the weatherbrown house
wading in waves of goldenrod and yarrow,
to country lanes beckoning through forgotten summers
across the borders of blackbird and wild grape,
to the guiding call of distant crow deep
within the timeless forests of the Cohannet and Assonet,
by the Council Oak, Anawon's Rock, and Metacomet's Cave,
(the arrowhead treasures hidden under the seasons)
by the sands of the Pokanoket, "bitter–water bays,"
ancient shores of the Mettapoisett and Pocasset.

Wuniish to rainy day adventures by the glowing hearth,

legends of our people, tales of Maushop, Wampanoag fables:
our little relatives in the waters, the woods, and the winds.

Wuniish to cool stables smelling of leather and dung,
to windstung iceboats slicing Winnecunnet Pond,
to the hot and salty climb for blueberries on Scargo Hill,
and braiding the sweetgrass from fiddlercrab marshland,
singing to the fish from a dory on the full moon tides,
speaking to the Sacred Rock from above the wrinkling bay,
leaving offerings at sunset in the burying ground by the lake,
that the Nobscusset old ones might know we remember.

Wuniish to the grumbling laconic humor,
to the wistful yesterdream remembrance of Grandmother,
to the whole simple, storied world that died
too soon and left him alone.

Wuniish to the boy
who found the visions of a people in Grandfather's eyes.
No one should think it strange that when I became a man
Grandfather and I together sought that boy and his dreams.
Now the grandfather is gone the boy will not be found again,
and only I am left to keep the visions and recount the dreams.

— Manitonquat

Contents

Prologue

It is cold today. There is no wind. The snow is hard as rock on the Burnt Church Reserve in the north of New Brunswick. Heavy gray clouds recline above the bony reach of the trees, threatening to deliver more snow. They seem to absorb both sound and time and seal the world into an eternity of winter.

Somewhere there must be a pale and distant sun beyond those clouds, lowering to the southwest, and near it the faintly traced circle of a new moon, for this is the time of mid-winter ceremonies. In the basement of the house of my friends gkeesettanamoojk and Lorna, the talking stick is passed around a circle of participants. Slow Turtle and I have driven twelve hours north from our Wampanoag country to mark this passage of earth renewal with our Wabanaki relatives. Some of the others here have come similarly long distances, from Maine, Nova Scotia, Quebec and Ontario. Opening prayers have been spoken to bring our minds together and remind us of our relationships to all of Creation. Each one in turn holds the stick and speaks. When that one speaks, all others still their noisy minds and listen with respect, with the heart.

A man is speaking. There is a shyness as he is not used to speaking before so many. He is not old, but hardship and suffering have made him cautious and circumspect.

"I am glad to be here. It is good to see so many have come from so far. I am glad that we still have some elders who take the trouble to come through this cold and share their knowledge with us. I need that. We have lost so much. Our people have lost so much, and still they hurt each other. I am a singer. I want to sing for my people in a good way. But others are so desperate they will sing in bad places just for money. It is no good to sell your culture. They do not understand. My family does not understand me. They hurt and blame each other. Our families are being torn apart. So now I am here. In this circle. Seeking the old ways that were good for our people. This circle is my family now."

He passes the stick. There is a silence between each speaker when the words and the feelings settle into each listener like a stone falling slowly to the bottom of a quiet lake. A man stirs the fire in the little potbelly stove and adds a few more sticks of wood. The next speaker clears his throat.

"This culture, the culture that was brought here and forced on us, it is not good for us. It is not healthy. See what it is doing to the world. I don't want my children to go to their schools. What do they learn there? They learn how to take drugs, how to get drunk all the time. They learn how to steal and lie. They learn how to disrespect women. They learn no pride in their own culture. They learn no honor for the elders and the old ways of our people. They laugh at them. This new culture is tearing our families apart.

"It's bad medicine. We take so much bad medicine. I used to be a drunk. I got drunk whenever I could. And I took drugs too. If you don't drink or take drugs people think you are a fanatic. They call you a square. But a cultural program helped me. It made me realize these are not our ways. They are bad medicine.

"Then I went to see Albert Lightning, the medicine man. I learned a lot. I learned how we tear ourselves apart. We pass on gossip that hurts people. Gossip is bad medicine. Then we hate ourselves. We look at ourselves and say, 'You look terrible.' That's bad medicine."

"That's right about our families," says the next speaker, a woman. "This is good, here. But how can we get our teenagers here? We have our elders here, and the parents and the little ones. But the teenagers don't understand this. There's all this peer pressure. My teenage son comes home drunk. I talk to him, and he listens. But he won't come here because his friends don't come. They think it's weird, you know. I talk to my daughter. She's married now, and working, trying to pay the bills. She says when does she have the time. She's in and out, on the run."

The stick passes to another woman.

"People can't see how important this is. It's important to our health. To our survival. We need these ways. This knowledge of how to live in a good way, how to be in harmony. I heard you tell stories before, Medicine Story. It was so good for me. Our stories are important. It is good you and Slow Turtle are here. Thank you for coming."

"I'm from James Bay, part Cree, part Inuit," a quiet man with a shy smile speaks. "I've traveled around a lot, heard a lot of people's stories. That's good. The Inuit have different stories. In the Inuit world there is no evil. Everything has a reason and a purpose. In the Inuit stories the first people were small and hairy. They lived like animals in lush jungles. Then the Creator made them different by giving them imagination. That's what made us different from the animals."

"I need to know who I am." Another woman speaks. "I always had strange feelings and dreams. They frightened me. I didn't talk about them, because I thought there was something wrong with me, but I can talk here in this circle. Here in the circle I feel whole. This is the first real harmony I ever felt with people."

The talking stick makes its way on around the circle bringing together inner thoughts and feelings that otherwise would have remained hidden. A man on a weekend pass from prison reminds us how many of our good people are taken from us. The road to prison is through alcohol and drugs, taken because of the oppression and despair of our people. Our people, the Indian people of North America, have the highest rate of alcoholism, the highest rate of suicide, the highest rate of unemployment, the lowest average income, and the shortest average life-span of any racial or ethnic group. The man from prison speaks about how finding the traditional ways has given him a positive image of himself, power and hope.

Now a non-Indian woman has the stick. She says that although she was invited, she feels a bit uneasy, not sure if she really belongs here. She wants to explain why she came.

"All people were once tribal people," she says, "but my people lost that way a long time ago. I think that it is a good way. I do not come looking for gurus. I know we must find our own way, but our communities and our families are disintegrating. Perhaps by sharing our thoughts and feelings we can help each other."

"You are welcome," an older man responds. "If you think you belong here, you belong here. Our way has never been to discriminate against others. It is too bad that people are sometimes so hurt they begin to hate other races and nations, but that is not our way."

That night we go to the school and have a dance. We are joined by the ancient sound of the drum. Coming late to the dance I stop outside to listen to the voices of the men, the women and children singing. Everything is so clear to me now. For our people, the answer to the problems of alcohol and drugs, of shattered families and generation gaps, of despair and lack of direction, lies in a return to the wisdom of our elders, to our traditions interpreted in a spiritual way — as universal principles to guide us in the world we inhabit today. Hearing the drum, feeling the heartbeat of the people, being borne through the stars by our patient, snow-clad earth, all is one harmony. Things are as they should be.

I stand there on the crunchy snow, breathing the sharp

*night air, listening, and watching the brilliant dance of the
stars in the deep black above. For thousands of years this
drum has beat, and the voices of the people have sounded together in the night. The dance has gone on.*

*How much longer will it continue? The old ways are
threatened, the people divided. Forces of destruction, of greed
and domination, are in subtle control of the governments and
institutions of the world beyond. It is fear, not love, that
makes this world go round today.*

*But the drum sounds in the hearts of all good people
everywhere. Our survival depends upon healing our circles.
The song is hope, harmony, beauty, healing, creativity. We
must carry it to the world. We must bring people back to the
circle. We need each other.*

Above, the stars continue the ancient round dance.

My mind recalls a meeting between some scientists and
Slow Turtle and myself. One of the scientists said they
needed help, and perhaps it was appropriate to ask the native elders, though he wasn't sure we would want to help
them. Slow Turtle told them the story of Passaconaway, famous medicine chief of the Penacook people of New Hampshire, who, when he learned of the invasion of the Europeans, foresaw great trouble for our people and for the earth.
So he went through a series of ceremonies to banish the
whites from these shores. When at last none of his rituals
affected the removal of the offensive intruders, Passaconaway
decided that Creator intended for them to come here to be
taught the ways of Creation. Unfortunately the Europeans
were not eager to be taught, and after Passaconaway left for
the Land of Souls, none of our other people were willing to
instruct those Europeans who seemed so deaf and blind to
Creation and the Creator's instructions for a healthy and
happy life.

Another scientist spoke saying he didn't believe that Indians or any other people had knowledge that could save the
planet. In his rational estimation this world was self–de-
structing at such an increasing rate he could only give it one
to ten years at best. Yet he said when he looked into the
eyes of his little granddaughter he could not bring himself to
think of her not having a life before her. And so, in spite of
all his misgivings, he sought hope.

Tonight, long after that meeting, I feel hope. It is the
hope I felt that night I want to share in the pages of this
book. Now I see that hope lies for all humankind in people's
awareness that the destruction of the earth and the ills of

society are all due to unhealthy attitudes fostered by unhealthy systems. I see that awareness beginning to grow. The
vision I was given when I started upon this medicine path
nearly two decades ago was that the hope of the world can
be found in the traditional wisdom of our elders, the old
ones of this continent. Now more and more people seek out
me and my brother and sister teachers — Slow Turtle, Oren
Lyons, Thomas Banyacya, Janet McCloud, Wallace Black Elk,
Sun Bear, Archie Lame Deer, and many more, who try to
show the hope that lies in a return to ways in harmony with
Creation: ways of respect, equality, freedom, cooperation, and
peace. These are ways that center on the family and the
clan, on hospitality, generosity, and the give–away.

It is hope that is my give–away wherever I travel. It is
hope, that I bring you here. Slow Turtle and I have taken
up Passaconaway's resolution to impart the instructions we
have received to all who will listen. In my travels I have seen
hope rekindled in many hearts that had been buried in cold
despair. I have seen hope born in people in prison, in people
controlled by alcohol and drugs, in people on the verge of
suicide, in people leading desperate, empty, meaningless
lives, lives of pain and loss. I have seen people listen to the
message I bring, and I have watched the light literally being
reborn in their eyes as they reached for my hand, or wept in
relief, as they chose life over death.

I have grown impatient, I fear. That scientist's dire predictions confirmed the need I feel to reach out further and
faster to more people. Through ten years of traveling I
thought about what I was learning, knowing that I might
someday put it on paper. For another ten years while I was
creating a community and teaching, I began to transcribe
those thoughts so that they might go out to those people I
would never speak with personally. From those twenty years
of work comes the book you now read.

Return to Creation is for human beings. At one time I
thought the teachings I was receiving would be for myself
and my nation alone. But over fifteen summers ago I had a
vision which told me clearly that the ancient knowledge still
held by our old ones was for all human beings, because we
are all tribal beings. This is part of the Original Instructions
of this Creation. It is encoded in our ancient memory and
passed through our genes.

Return to Creation is a book about the tribal way of life.
But, contrary to what you might expect from that, it is not

about the past so much as it is about the future. I hope to persuade you that, far from being archaic and anachronistic, the tribal way contains the best and perhaps the only hope for the survival of humankind.

Archaeologists have now discovered that millions of years ago in Africa old people were laid with their possessions in a community burying ground. This discovery suggests some very important things: that the earliest humans we know about took care of their elders, and interred them with respect in the earth. This does not paint a picture of a paranoid sub–human savage, snarling at his fellows and carrying off a kicking woman to his cave. Evidently these early humans had their customs and their ceremonies. They felt a connection to the earth and returned their bodies to her.

They lived tribally. These discoveries show that the human being is a tribal animal. There is a need for our species to associate with its own kind, to work and play together, to touch and be touched, to listen and be heard.

Over history, many people have left their tribes. Other tribes have dispersed. In many tribes today, many of the young people are no longer interested in the old ways of their people. They have turned away from the teachings of the elders and are much like young people everywhere else in the world. Modern consciousness calls this progress. But I see that this progressive society is actually built upon violence and greed. It creates loneliness and fear and alienation from people and from the world of nature. In modern cultures these feelings are so pervasive they seem to be normal, a part of being human.

But wherever I look at the life of traditional tribal peoples, I see that this is not their way. A small group of people committed to a relatively small area of land cannot afford to abuse each other or their environment; there is nowhere to hide from the consequences of their actions.

A few words about words. Some people object to the word "Indian." Of course, an Indian is from the country of India, and our people here got to be called that just because Columbus was lost. So then people say "American Indian" or even "Amerindian." That's not much better, and many who object to that use the term "Native American." But everyone born in America truly could be called that. "First People," or "Original People," or "Indigenous People" are better, but somewhat unwieldy.

There never was, before the invasion, a need for such a term. We were Pocassets or Assawompsetts or Pokonokets, or

Wampanoags, to distinguish us from other villages, areas, or nations. But now that all of us are a minority in our own lands we need to think of unity and communality. Since none of the names anyone has thought of to call us as a people seem just right, I use any and all of them at different times.

The word "tribe" also bothers some of our people, because it is associated in United States and Canadian history with misunderstanding and misuse. The word "tribe" comes from a division of ancient Romans, but it has long since been widened for many uses. Traditional people use the word "nation" rather than "tribe." This is a more accurate term, indicating the rightful place of these sovereign governments in the world family of nations. I employ the word "nation" in that context. But because there are many ways of organizing "nations" in the world, I use the words "tribe" and "tribal" to connote that form of nation in which the people have a close familial relationship to the land and to each other.

Another problem in the printed word is that of the gender of singular pronouns. Feminists have pointed out to us that there is a connection between male domination and the use of masculine gender words to denote both sexes together, as in "man" and "mankind." It is relatively easy to adjust that imbalance by using "people" and "humankind," but no one has found a universally accepted singular pronoun in English to connote both sexes. Some people have taken to writing "s/he," and other friends of mine are promoting a neologism, "cos." Both seem (perhaps in their newness) a bit stiff to me. My own response is to extemporize until the language of the people decides the issue, as it will some day. So sometimes I use "she" to add weight to that side and sometimes I use "he," eccentrically, just to create my own symmetry. If that confuses you, I think that is all right.

There is also an issue among our people about the value of writing. I am myself of two minds about it. I see that there is a great power in the oral tradition. No doubt we lose a great deal of mental ability and a quality of insight when we no longer have to store our most important knowledge in our own brains. As a keeper of oral traditions from my grandfather, I am very aware of their special nature. But the transmission of knowledge at this time is not just for pleasure or intrinsic edification; it is crucial to the survival of human life on the planet. I wish I could be everywhere. I wish I could sit with every person, every relative around the world, and speak of these essential things, the wisdom of our ancient heritage and how we must change ourselves and our society so that human life may continue and prosper. This book is my way of trying to do that.

You have come to the circle this book represents to hear me speak. Perhaps you wish to learn something about Native American healing from a medicine man. Maybe you wish to experience a healing yourself. Well, I hope you do learn something, and I hope you get in touch with the spirit of healing. I must tell you, however, that the healing power for you is only within *you.* A medicine person's real job, regardless of the medicine used — whether it be ritual, herbs, steam or water, song or dance or with story — is to convince you of your own healing power. That is the healing power of Creation which is within each of us.

I think our discussion here is important because in recent times there have been so many writings by non–Indian people full of foolishness about their supposed encounters with native medicine people. These books make our people laugh and shake their heads at the gullibility of a public that swallows such contrived nonsense. So before we begin perhaps I should dispel one expectation you may have.

People are always coming to me and asking me to teach them how to be a shaman. I often wonder what they think that really is. There is a tremendous fascination with shamanism these days, so strong it seems to stem from some deep need that people have. I believe that people today feel very helpless and powerless, and they are looking for short courses and quick cures to give them power. If I tell them it will take ten or twenty years or more to teach them what they want, they go away disappointed to look for a short cut. What they really want is to feel better about themselves, to feel like they are special, to be recognized as a somebody, somebody with special power. They don't realize they already are.

People really don't understand power. So they take martial arts classes, subscribe to get–rich–quick–in–real–estate–schemes, send for mail order courses and degrees, and plunge into all kinds of exotic spiritual disciplines and mind–training programs that promise to give them a handle to control a very confusing existence in today's world. I will discuss the issue of real power in a later chapter. For now I just want you to know that shamanism is not part of what I am concerned with here.

Perhaps you wonder why I don't want to be teaching something that is so popular these days. When I first was asked about shamanism, I questioned what it was. The word "shaman" comes from the old practices of Siberian natives. I don't know much about them, but I do know it is confusing to take a concept from one culture and try to apply it to others. It seems to me that people attracted by shamanism are looking for *magic*. People feel overwhelmed and threatened, and magic gives the promise of power and control. I guess that is the appeal of all these books about American Indian conjurers and sorcerers. Native people are not the ones who are buying all those books. It's not Indians you see running around out there in the deserts and mountains looking for *brujos*.

Most of these books are sheer nonsense, fiction disguised as sociology or biography or spiritual discovery. While the elementary spiritual ideas seem to be enlightening to some folks who have never been exposed to such thinking before, in light of the urgency of the dire situation in which we and all of humankind find ourselves, paying attention to these magical fantasies amounts to a frivolous digression. It is putting our heads in the sand.

Another hope I have for this book is that it may inform people of the great depth and wisdom of our native spiritual ways. For all my life I have heard people refer to the major religions of the world as Christian, Jewish, Moslem, Hindu and Buddhist. When I see ecumenical panels of religious leaders, they include people from some of these "major" religions but rarely a representative of native spiritual ways. When I have been asked to participate in such events or to speak of our ways, people always seem so surprised at the richness and depth of the wisdom our elders have preserved for us. That ignorance of our spiritual traditions, together with the belief that the Europeans had the only true religion, was what prompted the invaders to seek to convert us to Christianity and proscribe our ceremonies. People for whom religion is contained in a book and practiced in a certain building on certain days did not and do not understand a people for whom religion is in each individual heart and practiced at every moment in every place. Many of our people do not care to use the word religion for their own beliefs, because of what that word connotes in other cultures. Perhaps it is not appropriate for us, after all. The Latin roots of "religion" mean "to bind together again," and we have not ever felt separated from the Creation.

Return to Creation is a handbook of survival for native and natural people. I want to explain what those terms mean to me. Some people are both native and natural. That is, they live close to the earth, in spiritual harmony with its processes, in a community into which they were born that has developed a way of life that reinforces a commitment to the earth and to each other. Some people are native but not natural these days. In modern society there are tribal people who have lost that connection to their traditional land, who have been displaced to cities or other places of unnatural living conditions. Conversely, there are other folks who are natural but not native. That means they are not indigenous to the areas where they live, or their tribal allegiance has been lost, or they may be a product of racial and ethnic mixing, but they have gone back to the land and are creating a natural life style. This book is addressed to both native and natural people: to the indigenous people of the North American continent who seek to secure unity and respect for traditional tribal ways, and to non–native people who seek to create new tribes and live in a more natural and spiritual fashion.

As civilization has expanded it has eradicated many of the tribal peoples of the world by assimilation or genocide. Some people tend to talk as though that process has been completed, and is or was inevitable. Some people refer to native people in the past tense, even to my face: "The Indians had a good way of life," "It's too bad the white man had to destroy the red man." That kind of talk makes me a little nervous. Other people think the atrocities are all in the past, but the destruction of native lands and ways and peoples goes on today.

There is, however, a counter–trend, small as yet, towards not only the revival and re–integration of tribal nations, but also towards the creation of new tribes by people who have already seen the failure of both capitalist and socialist systems to provide a full and meaningful life for all people. These people see that tribal life provides the opportunity for greater harmony with the natural world, better relations with each other, and a healthier and more spiritual existence. One of the reasons I am writing this book is to provide encouragement and practical assistance to those involved in this movement. I do not advocate here that people go back to living in wetus or wigwams. I do not say they should throw away the great works of civilization in the arts and sciences. What I want to impart is a spiritual understanding. I want to explain the spiritual foundations of tribal living as I have come to understand them. Then I want to explore how these ways are affecting the lives of many people today, both Amerindian and non–Indian.

This spiritual knowledge is not specific to my religion. It is much older than all the world's religions. Understanding the Way of the Circle, of the relationship of all things, need not conflict with anyone's religion. It is the Way of Love, which is the basis of all the great world religions.

It is necessary here to confront a few myths that are propagated by schools, books, periodicals, motion pictures, and television. It is taught, and most people believe, that the indigenous people of North America were savage, brutal, warlike, hostile to strangers and cruel to each other. I call that the Big Lie, or turning the truth into its opposite.

In actuality, the people of this continent were among the most pacific, gentle and friendly people to be found on the planet. All of the initial encounters with Europeans were amicable. Our people welcomed the visitors and treated them with courtesy and respect. Hospitality was and continues to be one of the strongest customs of native people. It was only when the visitors began to take slaves and burn villages and steal land and cheat and dishonor their treaties that the natives began to suspect their guests' true intentions.

But what about all those Indian wars we always hear about? Well, in the first place, if you try right now to remember all the Indian nations with a warlike reputation, how many can you count? Mohawk, Huron, Sioux, Apache, Comanche. Perhaps Cheyenne, Arapaho, Crow, Blackfoot. Maybe you can add a few more. Maybe you'll come up with a dozen. Two dozen at the most, if you've read a lot. Very often these nations got that reputation after being attacked by the European invaders and pushed by those invasions into the territories of other nations.

In North America there were about five hundred different tribes, and the vast majority lived totally peaceful existences with no violence or hostility towards their neighbors.

As for the ways of the so–called "warlike" nations, I think that "war" is a very misleading word in this context. "War Game" would better describe the outings of warriors in these tribes. There were raids, typically for honor, or revenge, or women, later for horses. Among most warrior societies it was considered more courageous to touch an enemy and ride away than to kill him. These skirmishes had nothing to do with greed for land . Certainly they were nothing like the wars of conquest for territory and riches, slaves and religious subjugation that were the fashion of Europe and Asia. There were no crusades in America, no wars of succession, no Hundred Years War, no Thirty Years War, no Seven Years War among native tribes. If a war went longer than a day, it was too long. In the southwest, the very name of the people who have peacefully inhabited the mesas of northern Arizona, the Hopi, means "the people of peace," and they have been so from time immemorial.

The first peoples to ban war internationally as a method of resolving conflicts were on this continent. The League of the Houdenousonie, the Six Nations, is the oldest United Nations in the world, and the Great Peace they created by using words instead of weapons has lasted for a thousand years. Is it not time for the world to know this and to learn from the masters of peace?

There is another popular myth that says tribal life requires total conformity of the individual to the norms of the group, whereas free–enterprise capitalism fosters individuality. Again, this seems to be a reversal of the truth. It doesn't take very extensive observation to see the repressive conformity demanded by the dominant culture in this country. Nowhere is it plainer than in the fact that those who wear the wrong clothes or the wrong hair length, have same–gender sexual preferences, follow exotic religions, or espouse unorthodox political opinions are not acceptable in the mainstream of society. It is true that there was a greater cohesion to the spiritual traditions of the tribe among its members, but there was also a far greater tolerance of individual differences. Whether in a warrior, hunter, or medicine person, no dress or hair or paint or decoration or style of life was too outlandish to be accepted if this came from a personal vision. People of especially wild fancy, sexual deviants, dreamers, idiots, madmen and madwomen were looked upon affectionately and often treasured as holy beings.

The distinctions I make between the dominant and the tribal cultures, the preferences or prejudices that I may have concerning them, have nothing at all to do with race. Racism still colors too much of all our thinking. The racism of whites against people of color produces equally virulent racism against white people. But the oppression of human beings by other human beings has nothing to do with the color of their skin. In building a just and loving society, white guilt and red anger is not going to be helpful.

Wherever I go I always run into people who are surprised that I exist and that my people have survived. "I didn't know there were still Indians in the East," they say. Yes, twenty–five percent of the Indians in the United States are east of the Mississippi. Most people in Massachusetts don't know there are Indians in their own state. There are about eight thousand of us in the State of Massachusetts. People generally have the attitude that only people who are racially unmixed, or who have a certain percent of "pure Indian" blood can be considered Indians. The conquering governments make laws about that, but that is not our way. Because of the way that people of mixed blood are treated, I consider it rude and insulting for a native person to be asked how much of his blood is "Indian." All of it, I say. Are you a full blooded Indian, they ask? Of course, my blood is quite full, thank you.

We do not ask each other these questions. The blood of the Pokonoket runs in my veins. Swedish, Norman, Welsh and English blood also runs there, and I am proud of all of it. Our nations are not racial. They are a way of life and an inherited tradition. These ways and traditions are not well known. I learned nothing of them in my education in schools and university; I had to learn it all from my own people and from the old ones of other native nations.

Should the first people, the indigenous nations, succumb to the genocide of the "civilized" nations, that will signal the end of the human experiment on this planet. The lesson of our people is one of survival. Where we have survived, we have kept the spiritual foundations of our relationship to Creation intact. The dominant society today has the most horrendous tools of destruction, and at the same time the most compelling tools of communication. The violence, the oppression, the injustice are but hurtful remnants of our ignorant past. Existing alongside them are more people interested in peace, equity, and justice than ever before in human history; more people actively involved in building creative alternatives that are egalitarian and cooperative; more people trying to discover their essential humanness, to grow and to reach out to others.

Unfortunately, little of this has, as yet, found its way into the highest levels of power in the dominant cultures. But when the people know clearly what they want, they will be able to get it. This book is about finding your power and changing the world. You and I have the power to do just that, through our love, our intelligence and the power of our vision. I am only one person, you say. What can one person do? Mahatma Gandhi was only one person. Martin Luther King was only one person. It was the power of a common vision that Gandhi brought to India and King brought to black people in America.

It is a time to fulfill our dreams. We all know how it should be. Wherever I speak to people, on the streets, in schools, in the high offices of state, in prisons, at every level of society, people resonate with a vision of what Creation was meant to be.

Together we can weave the common vision of humankind. Together there is nothing we cannot do.

It is time for a Return to Creation.

Chapter One

The Magic Feather

You have come. That is good. We will sit together a while. You in the place where you are now, I where I am. I should like to be able to see your face. I should like to be rid of this barrier of paper and speak with you from my heart, to look into your eyes, to hear your voice and experience your heart. That is the kind of communication I am used to having with people. But since I cannot be with you just now, let us do the best we can and stay as open to each other as possible. I believe that we have common interests: an interest in life, an interest in health, an interest in peace, in love, in the beauty of earth, and in the rapture of consciousness.

Since you cannot hear my voice where you are now, I write down these words. As you read, your heart listens. I shall imagine you with me, and if you also imagine yourself here, we shall be together with our minds. As others read these words, we form a circle together. This is good.

We are on a great rock, large as a small hill, covering fully half an acre of ground. The top of the rock, where we are now, rises to the tops of the trees and the sun is warm upon the stone where we sit. This has been a gathering place for the Pokonoket Wampanoag for generation upon generation of our people. There are woods all around us still, and down the hill flows the Nemasket River, where once a village of our people stood.

Let us kindle a council fire at this time and put our minds together. I propose to have a number of such councils so that I may share with you some of the essential teachings of our old ones and consider how we may put such wisdom to work for us in the shrinking and dangerous world we share today.

I want to greet you all and thank you for coming. I want to ask that in this moment we put our minds together so that we may be of one mind. With one mind let us give our greetings and our thanksgivings to the earth, our common mother, from whom we are given all we need for living. With one mind let us give our greetings and our thanksgivings to all life upon the earth, our close relatives, who are bound with us in this great web of Creation. Let us expand our one mind together through the great universe beyond and give our greetings and thanksgivings to all the unknown beings beyond this tiny world. And let us with one mind give greetings and thanksgivings for the wonder of this life to the Power that created it.

What we need to investigate and learn together is healing: healing the earth, healing society, healing our communities, healing ourselves. In a time of great sickness nothing else should concern us. To paraphrase a saying, if we are not part of the medicine, we are part of the disease.

In order to heal, the causes of sickness must be diagnosed. The causes of the sickness of the environment, society, and individuals are all entwined. They are rooted both in the way we think about nature, society, and human beings, and in the institutions which shape our thinking and feeling. The great healing wisdom of the elders of this continent is not found in the practices of shamanism or magic or individual medicine, but in the spiritual ways of their society as embodied in the organization and daily life of the people. Native wisdom is not concerned with personal power or manipulation of the Creation. It is concerned with the circle, the whole, the family, the community, the nation, with humanity and all of life, with the earth and the harmony of the universe. It is that wisdom that I hope to help clarify here for all people of our time.

There is a rhythm to the universe. Part of sickness is losing the beat, falling out of time. That is why we use drums and rattles to heal. That is why we bring all of the universe into the medicine lodge. We sing the song that comes from within and without: the Song of Creation.

Sickness of any kind is a dissonance in the harmony of nature, a noisy intrusion into the Song of Creation. Of course, a certain amount of dissonance and conflict is expected and desirable as a spur to consciousness. Our most essential teachers are both Pain and Beauty. Without pain, which guides and corrects the course of awareness, there would be neither rapture nor ecstasy. But that pain, that dissonance, must only be a corrective, a quick alarm, and therefore brief.

The rhythm of the universe requires dissonant interruptions in the harmony of nature, and also moments of silence. We must be quiet at times so we can hear the music of the great silence.

A medicine person can be a guide, one who knows the back country of the mind and the pathways of the heart, one who has taken the journey of the spirit in other worlds and knows where these trails connect in the body and in the world of physical matter. Such a person can show you the routes, explain the safety precautions, and be a companion in your quest. But a guide cannot take your trip for you. A medicine person cannot see for you or hear for you or learn for you. In a sense a medicine person does not really teach or heal. A medicine person can only describe the territory, be with you and encourage you. You must learn for yourself. You must open yourself to your own healing.

Too many of us feel trapped and helpless, at the mercy of forces we can neither contend with nor comprehend. Part of my work as a medicine man is to reveal people's own healing powers to them, to help them understand the nature of the sicknesses that have overtaken the world until they now permeate all aspects of our lives. Another part is to illuminate your own vision by the light of the spiritual heritage of the ancient ones of this continent. This heritage contains all of the healing that is needed if life is to survive upon this planet that is our home.

The only magic I use in our gatherings here by the council fire is the magic of storytelling. In this magic we can bring our minds together to see with new eyes what kind of a life and a world we can make together.

There is a story among our people of Epanow, a sachem of Nope. Nope is an island of our people that later came to be named Martha's Vineyard, perhaps because the rich fruited hills reminded a sea captain of his daughter's vineyard in England. Epanow was the sachem, or chief, of the village of Aquinnah, named for the great cliffs colored with the four sacred colors of clay — red, black, white, and yellow — where the deity Maushop once lived and helped to create the races of humankind. This is still a place sacred to our people, and our village there is today called by the English name of Gay Head.

Epanow and his warriors were taken captive by the English during a trading–raiding expedition early in the seventeenth century. Epanow was very unhappy to be taken from his home, his family and his village. I guess the English must have thought the Indians would consider it a privilege to be shown their cities and their palaces, and to be paraded about as curiosities among the wealthy and noble of their society. Epanow had a difficult time explaining through a translator why he wanted so much to be returned to his home. But the sachem had powers other than speaking English.

While trying to explain his feelings to his captor, Epanow held out a turkey feather from his headdress. As the lord grasped the feather with Epanow, they both rose into the air and sailed out of the open window. They flew high above the clouds into the lands of the winds and the thunders, and then they swooped down over a green, wooded island riding in the silver sea. Over the hills and the trees they soared, over bounding deer and foxes, among the startled hawks and crows. They circled a small village of bark domes, saw the men fishing in the ponds, the women grinding corn, and the children running about. Everywhere there was song and laughter, both from the men and women working, and from the children playing.

They lighted in the center of the village, and the people all gathered around to welcome home their sachem and greet the honored guest. A great feast was prepared for the occasion, the singing society sang, the people danced in honor of the homecoming, and many tales were told by the *minatou*, the keeper of the lore. The sachem and his people were happy, but he could tell that the lord was unimpressed and somewhat uneasy. Epanow tried to think what would impress the nobleman, and then he remembered.

He held out the turkey feather again, and, grasping it once more, they were transported back to England, back to the palace and to the room they had left, seemingly many hours before. When the lord tried to tell the others in the room of all he had seen, they looked at him as though he must have gone mad.

"But, sire, you have only been standing a moment here

before us, holding on to that feather with your eyes closed."

"What sorcery is this?" the lord wanted to know. The translator explained that, since Epanow could not explain the beauties of his home, he had merely taken the lord into his mind to have him experience it as Epanow did.

Then Epanow spoke again. He said that in the lands to the west of his own island there was much of the yellow metal on which the Europeans seemed to set so much value, and if the lord would return Epanow and his warriors home on one of his ships, the sachem would show them where to find the gold.

As Epanow had guessed, greed sparked the venture, and soon the sachem and his men stood by the rails of one of the lord's ships, looking at the sacred cliffs of Aquinnah again. Epanow called out to his people below in their dugout canoes. He told them in his language to attack the bow of the ship and make a great commotion. As they did that, the sachem and his warriors watched for the lord's men to be distracted by the attack and then leapt overboard and swam to safety.

I can imagine the rejoicing and the feasting that took place when Epanow and his companions returned to their village. I can imagine the people asking the sachem what that strange place was like.

"This man lives in a great house, as big as our whole village," I can imagine Epanow saying. "There are many shining and beautiful things in that house," he would say, "and yet for all of that I did not see that the people there were as happy as our own people here in this village. The men and women did not sing as they worked. They looked with mistrust upon each other, and the truth was not in their speech. There were no children running under foot and laughing and shouting. And then I was taken to see the streets of their city. There was filth and disease and hunger everywhere I looked. These people allowed children of their own tribe to starve and elders to die in the gutters. I began to see that the people in the palaces lived so well because they took a little from all the others. As a sachem I would be ashamed to have more than any of my people and see them freeze and starve."

Epanow warned his people that the English would bring these ways into their land, and then a choice would come. I tell our people and all our little ones that they still have this choice before them today. A choice between the way of the dominant culture and the way of the tribe. A choice between a way of exploitation and contention and greed, of rich and

19

poor, of pollution and disease, of apathy and indifference and cruelty, or a way of sharing and caring, of simple living close to the earth, in appreciation and respect and love.

I tell you this story today to say that the choice is still ours. It is a very real choice, and it is available to you and to me right now, at this very moment and at every moment of our lives.

To understand the choice, we must first speak about such subjects as the meaning and purpose of Creation, of Life and Intelligence. The most essential ingredient of a healthy and vigorous individual, community, society or world, is a strong spiritual center. For the strength of our communities, we need to come together often to share our spiritual concerns.

I often say that there are two kinds of people in the world — the ones who say there are two kinds of people in the world, and the ones who don't. Obviously, I am one of the former. Some of the people who share our earth believe there is some sort of Intelligence that has ordered Creation, and others don't. In my view spirituality is not divisible or exclusive, and our spiritual agreements must include all of us. This is not easy when so many refuse to be included in any grouping of the family of humankind. But they are brothers and sisters even if they deny it, and we cannot throw anyone off the world or out of our hearts.

It is human to want order, to desire beauty, to seek meaning. If you believe there is an intelligence and an order to the universe, then your job as a human being is to discover them and follow them. If you believe there is no order or purpose to the universe, then your job is to create and supply them. It amounts to the same thing, provided the jobs are done with a pure heart and a clear mind.

H umankind has a long history of arrogance. The oppressive and hurtful institutions by which men dominate other men, women, young people, and all of nature, create feelings of superiority and arrogance. The spiritually arrogant think they alone know the way of Creation. That certain knowledge has created all our divisive sects and religions — "My savior is greater than your savior, my scriptures and stories are older and holier than yours, my path is the only true path." The mentally arrogant, who can be found by the multitudes in our political and scientific histories, believe that they know how to order and rearrange the universe. Such thinking has now brought us to the edge of extinction's abyss.

The common denominator that we all share is life, so we can speak of these things together. But before we speak of such things it is the custom of our people to purify our bodies, minds, hearts and spirits of conflicting, disruptive elements. We do this through what is called in my language the *pesuponk*, or sweat lodge ceremony. In this ceremony we try to establish through supplication and meditation — often called prayer — a communication with the powers of Creation that lie within and without.

Let us take Epanow's way of the magic feather. I reach out my feather to you from this page. If you would grasp it with me, we may journey together.

Take hold of the feather now and come with me to the pesuponk, the place of purification.

Chapter Two

Pesuponk

We stand now on the shore of a small river that winds through woods and marshes to a large bay, one of the many arms of the great sea that embraces our lands. This is the country of the Wampanoag, the People of the Dawn, the Children of the Morning Light.

It is possible you may never have heard of the Wampanoag Nation before now. It was never a very large nation like some of the famous ones you have heard about, rather it was a collection of villages shifting about the shores and woods of southeastern Massachusetts. The villages that bordered the lands of the Narragansett and the Massachusett often banded together for mutual interests. A strong sachem that could coordinate trade and defense might become the massasoit, or great leader of the nation, but how often and how far he would be supported and followed depended on the sachems and councils of the individual villages.

On Cape Cod and the islands off the Cape, the tribes were the most secure and therefore the most independent. On the river bank where now we stand there was once a village that continued as an Indian community until the early part of this century when the native inhabitants diffused into the town of Dartmouth and imploded again into the centers of New Bedford and Fall River. This land from Narragansett Bay to Buzzard's Bay was known to our people as Pokonoket, land of the salt–water bays, and contained many villages.

In the side of the river bank is a small cave that has been dug out by the young men of my nation. Over the entrance is a covering of canvas and blankets. A few feet in front of it is a small mound of earth and a few feet beyond is a pit in which a pile of small rocks is enveloped in flame. A young person of my nation stands there, tending the fire.

I explain to you that even though you may have been in other sweats, the ways of different nations are different, and the ways of different leaders in the same nation may also be different. The ways of my sweat are my own vision, my own adaptation of the ways of my nation.

The pesuponk is ready now, so we take off all our clothes and crawl in through the small low door and sit on the damp ground. I sit at the back, facing the pit in the center and the door beyond. Our fire–keeper fills the pit with glowing rocks from the fire, one by one. We bless each rock as it comes in with a bit of cedar leaf which smokes and fills the lodge with its sweet and pungent aroma. The fire–keeper closes the door and seals it with earth so that no light may enter.

Here we are in the dark now. If you are an American Indian this experience may not be strange to you, for it is a universal purification performed by traditional peoples all over North America. But if you have never been in an Indian sweat lodge, no words of mine will convey to you how it feels to be here. If you sit on the earth cross–legged, or hunched over with your knees together, and close your eyes, you can imagine the dark. If you have ever been in a sauna or steam bath you can imagine the heat. But you cannot imagine the spirit of the pesuponk, the spirit of the rocks and the fire, the water and the steam, the disappearing of time, and the returning of Creation to our consciousness.

Although I will tell you what is happening, you will not know or understand the full meaning and impact unless you have had, or until you have, a sweat yourself. You may have had a sauna, but that is very different, according to the people from Finland who have been in my sweat lodge. A sauna is good, it is healthy, but it purifies only the body. You may even build an Indian sweat lodge, but unless you build it with a spiritual awareness, totally conscious of the gathering of the wood and rocks, of the building of the fire, as well as of the lodge, and unless you perform the ceremony in a sacred manner, you will not achieve the purification we now seek of body, mind, heart and spirit. If you are careless and inconsiderate, you can do yourself much harm, for the power of this way is great.

That is why many of our people have expressed concern about non–Indians making their own sweat lodges. It is not because we think this way is only for Indian people. It is because we have been afraid the way might not be fully appreciated and respected, and therefore, people might cause themselves harm. It was this concern that prompted some of my elders many years ago to instruct me to explain our ways to any non–Indian people who were interested enough to want to know about them. As I have spoken of this way in many places around the world since then, I have found that using steam for healing is very common and very ancient on this planet. At one time, all the uses for steam healing were spiritual, but these ways were lost to people as they were converted to other religions. Because of this I believe the sweat is for all people, not just for my people. I do not think that others should do it in my way, but should find their own ways.

The rocks glow red in the pit, a pulse of heat in the center of our dark little universe. Only the familiar, cool earth under us maintains a contact in our consciousness with the everyday world of matter and life which we have left behind. I begin to speak in the old language of our people. I drop one small piece of sage on the rocks. The fumes embrace our nostrils and enter our bodies. (We have no sage in this part of the country, but I know our ancestors used this in the west before the eastern migration, so I always pick some when I go through the western mountains.) With a sprig of cedar I dip into the herb water I have prepared and splash it on the rocks. A fierce wave of concentrated heat strikes out at us, and we gasp at its intensity.

Now I explain in our common language of English that I have used the old tongue because that is what the ancients who preserved this pesuponk for us would understand, and if any of these ones are listening, I wish them to know that I remember them, that I am grateful that they lived in a good way and taught their children well, so that their good ways would not be lost to us.

I explain that I have first of all thanked Kishtannit, the Creator, for showing to Maushop this way of cleansing ourselves and getting rid of our poisons, and I have thanked Maushop for showing it to our people, and Weetucks for reminding the people to follow this way when they had

forgotten. I then gave greetings and thanksgivings to Mettanokit, our Sacred Mother the Earth, and to all of her
children, ourselves and our relatives the animals, the trees
and grasses, even the rocks radiating in the center of the
pesuponk. I gave greetings and thanksgivings to Potanit,
spirit of the fire, that has entered our rocks and filled them
with its energy, to Paumpagussett, spirit of the great waters
of life that we administer to the burning rocks, and to
Tashin, spirit of the winds that carries the purifying steam
onto and into our bodies, our minds, hearts and spirits. I
have given greetings and thanksgivings to Keesuckquand,
Grandfather Spirit of the heavens, whom we see in the
person of Nepaushet, the Sun, and to his wife and sister
Nanepaushet, our Grandmother, the Moon, who guides the
cycles of purification, of creativity and fertility, and to the
Nucksuog, the unknown beings of the star nations beyond. I
have thanked and greeted the spirit of the pesuponk and all
the other spirits of the place where we are and everywhere in
the universe.

The way that I conduct a sweat ceremony derives from
the old story of how Maushop gave this way to the people.
As Creator's helper, he had worked on the fashioning of the
bodies of human beings out of the four colors of clay in the
sacred cliffs of Aquinnah. Into their skulls, which he made
from living trees, he put minds which could help them create
houses and spears and canoes. Into their breasts he put
hearts to guide them through the knowledge of love and
beauty, and, finally, he put some of the Creator's spirit to
give them life.

His twin brother, Matahdou, also gave gifts to these
human beings, but because his mind was distorted with
jealousy toward his brother, his gifts were not so good. They
were in fact four poisons, one specific to the body, another
to the mind, another to the heart, and one to the spirit. To
cleanse them of Matahdou's poisons, Maushop's subsequent
inspiration was to have the human beings construct a small
universe, into which they would bring everything in Creation
in the form of rocks, which had been infused with the energy of Creation in the form of fire. Onto the fire they would
pour water, the essence of life, creating a healing power of
steam. The humans would also invite the healing powers of
the four directions to help them rid themselves of these four
poisons.

When I conduct a sweat, first I invite us to give our
attention to Nanummy–in, that spirit being of the north,

there behind where the men are sitting, whose color is white,
the color of cleansing and of purification. This is the one
that sends the cold winds of winter. To this one we will pray
for help in sweating away all the poisons of our bodies, and
to give to ourselves, our families and our nation, bodily
health, strength and endurance.

As I throw more water on the hot rocks, we breathe the
healing steam deep through our nostrils, deep into our
lungs. We feel the cleansing strength in our sinuses, in our
throats and bronchial passages. The spirit of the steam
enters our blood, cleanses and strengthens our hearts, our
veins, capillaries and arteries, and all the living cell spirits of
our bodies. The toxins and tired waste in the blocked places
are dislodged and flow out of the body through the returning
breath and the perspiration that pours freely from us now.

At this time we can also send a healing to all those who
are not in the pesuponk with us today. In this circle we
have much power. If we all think of a person who is sick
and send the spirit of the steam, it will reach anywhere on
the earth. People who have been in the sweat with me have
reported amazing cures of distant relatives and friends right
at the time we sent the healing. One woman in the hospital
had a tumor that began that day to go away, and she did
not have to have an operation. The uncle of another person
gave up drinking the same afternoon that we prayed for him
to be rid of his disease of alcoholism. I have had too many
such reports for me to believe them just coincidences. We
are dealing here with a very strong power. We must use it
carefully and wisely.

Now we give our attention to Wampanand, the healing
power of the east, over there where the door is, spirit of
the dawn, of the renewal, of spring, whose color, like the
energy of the returning sun, is yellow. This one is the guardian of our people, and we see this light to our lives as the
Cosmic Intelligence. To this one we will pray for help in
sweating away the poisons of the mind. What are the poisons of the mind? Whatever is untrue. All of the beliefs,
defenses, rationalizations and other self–deceptions by which
we try to seem greater and more clever than others, the
pretenses and masks we fabricate, the scales and the judg-
ments by which we put others beneath us.

The reasons for all of these negative, untrue thoughts,
comes from one big lie, the greatest falsehood of all, the idea
that there is something basically, essentially wrong with us
— that part of our very nature is evil and bad. It is taught

to all of us by the dominant culture in many ways when we are very young. There's something wrong with you, as a child, as a boy, as a girl, because you are lazy, selfish, stupid, because you are weak and ignorant, because you are quiet or loud, because you are red, black, yellow, or white, tall, short, chubby, skinny — whatever you are, it's wrong. Those are all lies. The Creator made no evil. Every baby born is good, lovable, loving, intelligent, beautiful, special and wonderful. That's who you really are. Those other thoughts are all lies.

These poisons also include our desires: all the things we think we need, that we have been programmed to believe we must have in order to be happy, all those things that disturb the clarity and tranquility of our minds. They include our conditioned thinking — the belief that our labels are real; that the ways of our species, our race, our nation, our community, are superior to the ways of other peoples; that our children are foolish, our old people out of touch, and the opposite sex inferior.

We must let the steam enter into our minds and let all of that go. We must release those insistent lies that tell us we are not much good, that we are not intelligent, capable, beautiful and lovable individuals. We have to get rid of those persistent negative thoughts. We must return our brains to the condition of the sharp, reliable instruments the Creation gave to us when we were born and means for us to have now. As the steam rises once more from the rocks we pray for clarity and honesty.

We turn now towards Sowanand, behind where the women sit, that red spirit of summer that rides with Towuttin, the south wind, and tends the lodge of the heart. The poisons of the heart are all the bad feelings that take up residence there. Bad feelings have their purpose. Fear helps us to survive. Grief allows us to experience love in times of loss. Anger generates action and solves difficulties. But when we do not express these feelings fully, they cling to us and can stay stuck inside us for years, distorting our thinking, making us confused and numb. Now is our chance to get rid of our buried feelings, of anger, frustration, hate, envy, jealousy, resentment, hurt, anxiety.

My grandfather taught me that all of our bad feelings are the children of only one — and that one is fear. Now as the steam enters our consciousness in the silence, in the darkness of our ignorance and fear, we let it search out the bad feelings that lurk within us. When we discover a bad feeling we hold on to it for a moment, to feel it and to know it, until we know that we do not want to hold on to that feeling any longer and can let it go. This feeling has been hiding inside us and does not want to leave. We need to feel its hurt another time to want to be rid of it. When the water hisses on the rocks again we let it go, the anger born of fear, the frustration born of fear, the envy born of fear, the greed born of fear, we cast them all out — all the children of fear. They burst from us with a cry or a sob, a shout, a howl or a sigh, and evaporate in the healing steam.

F inally, I invite us to turn our attention toward Check-suwand, that black being there in the west, behind where I sit, for this is the one to help cleanse our spirits. Everything in the universe has a spirit, a consciousness of itself. This includes every atom and each particle of every atom, as well as the molecules formed by these atoms. It also includes every cell in our bodies; each one has its own spirit and its own consciousness. Together all our cells make up the little universe we call ourselves, the totality of body, mind, and heart which also has a spirit, that which some people call soul. Consciousness is not only in our minds, it is in each cell of our bodies. Our totality includes an external consciousness, a universal conscious-ness which is the Way of Creation, the Force of Life, work-ing through us.

Our spirit can be affected by the body, mind and heart, as well as by the ways in which we interpret the experience and environment of the self. This is what we try to express with such terms as "in good spirits" and "low in spirit," and so on. The great poison to the spirit that is the self is the illusion of separateness. At one time human beings knew, as our animal relatives and our plant relatives still know, that we are all part of one organism, the universe. When Matahdou brought poison to humankind, it included a sense of isolation, a way of making the self feel separate in a hostile and alien universe. I think this isolation is the feeling that has produced both the great arrogance of the human species, and its great fear of death.

In order to sweat away this poison we need to remove our consciousness from our bodies, from our thoughts and feelings. We need to die, to put time behind us, to face Death, to greet and know the other side of Life. Death guards the lodge of Life. To enter the lodge, to live fully and consciously by the fire of Life, we must make friends with the Dark One who waits outside by the door.

The great monuments to greed, the lust for power of our species, the wars and conquests, the exploitation and colonization, the palaces and prisons, the pollution and garbage of a riotous and desperate materialism, the pomp and circumstance, the hierarchies and bureaucracies, the honors, stardom, prizes, awards, medals, degrees and titles that people covet, all these seem but pitiful, vain, and self–deceptive attempts to avoid or to conquer the Enemy, Death. We see Death as the slayer of the self we have come to feel is alone and separate and tragically temporary in the vastness of eternity.

The more we cling to the close and familiar, the greater grows our fear of the unknown. We do not wish to look outside the lodge of Life into the darkness beyond. So we clutter our environment with possessions to distract ourselves, and we sing very loudly in the hope that our song will not be forgotten. Surely no one as important as we think ourselves to be can be obliterated! But deep inside we know the vanity of our posture, the inadequacy of our gesture. And so we are anxious, dissatisfied. We are not whole. We are not at one with Creation.

This is the time to greet the Dark Being. To look outside into the long night of eternity. To consider the inconceivable mystery of existence. To think of our ancestors who tried to learn and to live in balance, and who passed what they learned to their children. Here I think of my own nation that rose from the sea, sailed from the islands, lived under the earth, crossed the floods and the deserts and the ice and mountains and plains until they found the shores of dawn where our people have lived now for some ten thousand years. Remembering, I sing the song of the wolf, our ancient teacher, that song we brought to remind us of the ties and duties of families and tribes. I remind myself of the unborn generations to come, of whom we are the ancestors. These generations will not know the ways of the old ones unless I remember and teach them. I remember that everything in the Creation is equal, that I am a relative to all that is, that my family is everywhere, not only in the lodge of Life. The Dark Being is my relative too. We are bound in love.

Now we will sit in the silence, in the dark. We will give everything to the pesuponk. More water, more steam, hotter and hotter. Our shells are shedding. Here in the womb of eternity we cast off the husks of our contrived selves and become again pure seed, the potential of unlimited creativity. This is the time now for each of us to meditate, to express ourselves in prayer or song, however the spirit inclines us.

Now is the time of rebirth. I remind us all to leave our womb quietly, as gently and respectfully as we wish our own birth could have have been. I remind us to thank our relatives, all of Creation, as we go. We move very slowly, crawling into the light, wash our bodies, and sit or stand or lie quietly for a time. We are in a very delicate and vulnerable condition, soft and tender as newborns. If we move too fast we may faint or stumble. Our spirits and energies are very diffused now, spread out through time and space. If we shout we will dissipate more energy, and we could attract confused spirits to us before our earth sense and life force have fully returned. We must quietly assimilate the powerful experience we have just had . . .we feel very light, very expanded, very joyous, very loving . . .our bodies are completely relaxed, our minds clear and peaceful . . .we are full of air and floating. . . .

Now we are ready to come together and share our concerns, our dreams and visions, our hopes, our songs and stories, and our love.

Chapter Three

Return
to
Creation

*I lie with my back upon the earth. I feel the cool healing
earth power being drawn into my heated body after the sweat
bath. I rest deeply, supported securely on the bosom of the
Mother as she turns me toward the Father. The blue depth of
my Sky Father's mind absorbs my own mind. A few frail
puffs of cloud fleet across his face like quizzical expressions.
The salt wind from the low tide flats sighs through the marsh
grass and rustles the silver poplars in a glimmering dance.*

For a while, after the pesuponk, it is good to stay quiet
and be alone with nature. It is good to lie flat on the ground
and feel the strength of Mettanokit, our sacred Mother, the
earth, radiating her healing energy through our cleansed
bodies, filling our thoughts and feelings with her beauty.

Pesuponk has relieved us of the burden of being individuals in a certain place and time. In the darkness the
walls of our universe expand outward forever. Our bodies
continue to feel the reassuring stability of the earth supporting us as our spirits return to them under the patient gaze
of Nepaushet Kesuckquand, our Grandfather Sun.

The earth seems totally good. The grass, the trees, the
rocks, the sand, the river, the ocean, the clouds, the winds,
the seagulls, terns, and cormorants sailing and dipping
though them — all these seem connected, and I am connected to them all.

My body dries warmly with the caressing rays of Nepaushet, glowing golden beyond the sky. What a marvel that
it is there, close enough to keep me from freezing, not so
close as to burn me up! What a marvel that it exists at all!
What a marvel that the earth exists, and that life exists
upon it! What a marvel that I exist and think these
thoughts! What a marvel that anything exists, that there is
a universe of billions of galaxies with billions of stars and
billions of planets in each, and no doubt billions of life
forms all struggling to survive and become more conscious.

It is very mysterious. There it is. A vast universe, space,
energy, matter, all connected and all following the same
natural law. Everything has found a place in it. And here we
are, tiny humankind, one of millions of species of living
creatures on one little speck of dust, wondering what our
place is and doing some strange things with the brief time
of our individual lives: creating death, creating violence,
creating famine, creating hatred, loneliness, fear and sickness.

How strange! Pondering the stars, the sun, the earth, the
winds and waters and all the other living creatures, I note
that everything is working together in a wonderful way. A
feeling of perfect trust in Creation pervades my whole being.
I have no trouble finding my own path in all this.

But then I look at the human beings, beings capable of
love, of beauty and joy. I see humans wrapped in fear,
mistrust, and hopelessness. They are angry and frustrated,
pursuing self–destruction and destroying the earth along
with them. What an irony that a creature of such intelligence and creativity can appear so stupid and destructive!

I recall that the stupid, destructive history of this species
is still very recent. For most of the million or more years
that human beings have existed, they have lived in harmony
with the natural laws. For most of that time they lived in
small circles we call tribes and took care of each other and
their environment. They sang and danced and told stories.
Even today in those few areas where civilization has not
brought its attendant oppressions upon the natural tribal
peoples, they still live that way, close to each other and the
natural earth cycles.

In order to consider the complicated causes of the destruction we see today, we need to get in touch with the
basic reliability of the universe. We need to experience that
simple feeling of rightness that attends our contemplation of
existence apart from the confusions of human activity. When
we do so, the understanding that pervades our perception of

Creation is one of trust.

Trust.

It is a lack of trust that lies behind all the destructive behavior of human beings: the wars, the crime, the greed, the suspicion, the barriers, the isolation, the hurt, the inability to love. All of these begin in fear: the fear of not surviving or of not getting enough, the fear of dangerous and malevolent forces one perceives at work in the universe, the fear that beneath the sweetness lurks the truth of poison and evil. From a human perspective what we need to know is if the Creation is benign or malignant. Is there safety in it?

There is a story that is told. The Hobomock, or Hobomocko, was a spirit, one of the myriad spirits existing in the outer universe while the stars were made. He was one of the starmakers. There were spirits of all kinds, all different. Hobomocko's difference was this: he was filled with doubt. I will not say it was fear, for who knows what a spirit may fear? But Hobomocko doubted that everything was all right. He doubted that the universe was friendly. He felt there was something wrong, something missing in Creation.

Since the Creator, Kiehtan Kishtannit, made no mistakes, and since the Creation is perfect, it also must have been perfect for there to be one spirit who felt this way and was not content. All kinds of consciousness had to be available in this universe, and it was Hobomocko's lot to have this one. Some of our people have called the Hobomock the Evil One, but there cannot really be evil in a perfect creation. Evil is an illusion. The illusion that there is really something fundamentally wrong in Creation. That sense of evil, of wrongness at the very heart of Creation, strikes terror in our souls.

It was Hobomocko who whispered to Matahdou, Maushop's twin, when they were in the womb, that Matahdou should be the firstborn and who made him jealous of Maushop. (Jealousy is fear, the fear you are not all right and won't get what you need, or will lose everything.) Later, while making himself into the form of a great snake, the Hobomock whispered to Cheepii, a man of Nope, that there was not enough, and that the world was a dangerous place, with evil lurking everywhere. Then Cheepii thought, if Kiehtan the Creator didn't make any mistakes, then how is it that he made a spirit like Hobomocko who goes around saying that everything is a mistake?

So Cheepii became afraid. When he became afraid he became angry. He told our people that Hobomocko was the Evil Spirit, and that Kiehtan had made a mistake in making him. He said that Kiehtan could not be trusted, and the universe was unsafe.

And Hobomocko the Serpent was glad of being feared and hated. It made him feel that he was right. But even those who are glad to be feared and hated are not evil. They have their place in the lessons of Creation.

At first Cheepii created confusion among our people. They began to be afraid. Some took to magic to get more and to protect themselves, thus increasing the reality of Hobomocko by believing him. Others began to steal or kill to get more. This made everyone afraid of each other, and since they no longer shared with and loved one another they began to be sick.

Many of the sick came to Maushop to be healed, and he took them into the pesuponk. There he saw the error that was causing them to fear. He saw that the idea had come to their minds that Creation was not perfect and that Hobomocko was evil.

He told them this was an illusion. He said this fear was not born in the heart, but in the mind, in false ideas. He said our hearts know the true from the false.

When we feel good we are always loving, and that is real and true. When we feel bad, that is fear, a shadow, the unknown. It makes us act in foolish and unloving ways.

Maushop said we must follow the Path of the Heart, which is the Path of Beauty.

Whatever fills our hearts with the joy of love and beauty is the true way of Creation. Those who fear and those who are glad to be feared show us that they do not know the way of Creation, for without love there is no true joy. The fear and the mistrust are there as a lesson for us all to see. So the people began to believe in the goodness of life again, and in the goodness of themselves and each other. Harmony returned to our people, and Cheepii went away to try and find other people to frighten with his doubts.

Our people never saw him again. But we think he must have found others to convince, because about four hundred years ago a load of boat–people landed on our shores, dressed in black and talking about sin and damnation and the devil.

Without trust there can be no knowledge. We have to believe in the reliability of natural law in order to make predictions. If we cannot predict, we cannot plant seeds or gather medicines. Prediction is grounded in trust.

So is prophecy.

Take a little journey with me now. Take the magic feather, and we will rise together and soar above the forests here of pine and oak. There below us are the lands of the Pokonoket Wampanoag, the woods, the beaches, the bays, the rivers and lakes where once were the villages of the Acushnet, the Sakonnet, the Pocassett, the Mattapoisett, the Assawompset, the Nemasket, and the Assonet. There is Lake Watuppa where some of my forebears lived, and just above it our Watuppa Wampanoag Reservation where we have many ceremonies during the year. Beyond is the wide reach of the Taunton River, which our people knew as the Titticut, a major waterway for us, proceeding north from Fall River. We will come down on Assonet Neck that narrows the river a little beyond Assonet Bay. There is a state park with a little building that houses and protects a large rock.

This is known as Dighton Rock. There are marks carved over all of one side — the side that faces the river. There are many theories about these petroglyphs saying that they were made by Vikings, Portuguese explorers, even Egyptians. There are dozens of theories. Of course, our people know they were made by our ancestors, but theories seem to keep the scholars and hobbyists happy, so we let them alone. They never ask us anyway.

There have been additions over the years, but the basic message was set into the rock a long time ago by a prophet of our people. His name was Weetucks.

At that time, it is said, our people had begun to fall away from the Original Instructions explained to them by Maushop who had departed, many millennia before. He had come to feel that the people depended on him too much and that he was impeding their growth. So he called them to-gether and told them they must assume responsibility for each other, for the Earth Mother and all their relatives, the children of the earth. Then he went away towards the rising sun, there to remain until the world's end.

Some of our people feel that end is soon to come.

After many thousands of years the people had become confused because they had neglected the ceremonies and forgotten the stories and the knowledge that Maushop had taught them. They had forgotten all about the pesuponk. The people were quarreling again, and seeking magic because they were afraid. They forgot to care for each other and began to gossip and to quarrel.

There was a young widow who became pregnant and would not say who the father was. People were superstitious. They thought the father might be a magician or a demon, and they shunned her. She lived in the forest, some distance from the village, and kept to herself. When the baby was born it was a boy, and she called him Weetucks. The boy grew very quickly and soon was helping his mother, hunting and fishing and repairing the lodge.

When Weetucks was about twelve years old and coming of age, he told his mother that it was time for him to seclude himself alone for a time, in the traditional way. She did not know how he knew this, for he never went into the village or talked to anyone, and anyway the people had all forgotten about such ways.

He was gone for the turning of a moon. People thought he was lost or hurt and searched for him. When he returned he went straight into the village and collapsed on the water path. He was covered with dirt, for he had buried himself in the earth to receive knowledge from the Mother. And he had been on a mountain top to receive knowledge from Father Sky, from Grandfather Sun, from the winds and the distant stars.

When the village people saw Weetucks covered with dirt they knew that he had been given his direction on the medicine path. For they remembered that to go back that way into the heart of the Mother and receive her teachings was the traditional beginning of such a journey. When this occurred with no instruction from an elder it meant that the knowledge came directly from Kiehtan, from the Creation itself.

So they knew this boy must have a special knowledge, and when he spoke they came and listened. He spoke of the old ways, though he had been taught them by no man or woman. He taught them about the Original Instructions of the Creator. He spoke of Maushop's teachings, of the ceremonies that had been forgotten and how they should be done. He showed them again how to heal themselves in the sweat lodge and mud bath ceremonies. He spoke of healing herbs and other knowledge. Some of these things are well-known now, and others are closely guarded secrets to be known and used in a sacred manner only by our medicine people.

He was visited one night by two spirit guides from the place of the departed ones, who came to take his mother back on the Star Path to the Land of Souls. At that time they spoke to him of the things that would happen to the land and her people in times that would come. When the ceremonies for his mother had been completed, Weetucks gathered all the people to tell them of the prophecies he had been given. He said that Hobomocko's whisper of fear would one day spread across the world, and it would bring disease, violence, and starvation over all the earth. Many would die in confusion and ignorance, but those who remembered the sacred teachings, the Original Instructions, would be able to save their children and heal the earth. Many would lose their way, take a wrong turning, leave the sacred path, yet they would still be able, if they understood in time, to retrace their steps and return to the way of Creation. Those who returned to Creation would raise their children in the right way. These children would begin a whole new world, a world in harmony with all Creation, a world of people guided only by their heart's joy in love and beauty.

He showed the people the rock on which he had carved the story of the Great Spirit creating and giving instructions to all beings. On the right side are two human beings at the culmination of Creation, one listening and returning upon the sacred path, and the other preparing to continue on a path that leads to his own destruction, shown by a bolt of lightning ready to strike. This was the last message of Weetucks. There was a great feast. Many people had come to hear the prophecies, including the Turkey People from across the bay, who had sometimes been enemies, but now made a new peace with our people. The celebration lasted all through the night with much rejoicing and merriment. Before dawn the people followed Weetucks to the shores of the Turkey Bay where he bade them farewell. As the sun rose behind them, Weetucks walked across the waves towards the western heavens and was never seen again.

I t's a curious fact that the Hopi people of the southwest also have an ancient carving of prophecy on a rock and its message is much the same.

That is what the carvings on Dighton Rock are really about, unknown to all the scholars and archaeologists. That is not all of the message of the rock, but it is not time now to reveal more. I am instructed to tell this part of the prophecy now, as it is in keeping with other prophecies of the peoples of Turtle Island, such as the Hopi message of the Great Purification, the Lakota story of the Great Buffalo, and the Anishnabe prophecies of the Seven Fires.

These prophecies are being told now because it is believed that some will hear and heed. Some from every race and nation will begin to retrace their footsteps and find the sacred path again.

For any of you who may find it hard to believe such old tales from a people who are strange to you, let me speak briefly about the 1968 report of the Club of Rome. This club is comprised of scores of the foremost scientists of the world, from every area of learning, who studied the trends of the first six decades of the twentieth century and projected them into the future. This scientific prophecy reads just like our own. Famine, disease, violence, all increasing in our lifetime into the greatest destruction humanity has yet experienced, more devastating to more people than the fire, the ice, or the floods of past eras. Scientist Isaac Asimov wrote in an editorial in his magazine a few years ago, that he thought we had a less than fifty percent chance of surviving the next thirty years.

But you can be your own prophet. Look at what is happening today in the world all around us. Topsoil is washing away, water tables are receding under the earth. Water and air are becoming more polluted. There is acid rain and a hole in the ozone layer. This is the first time since this world was formed that the relationship between the earth and the sun has been changed, and it changes more each day. Population is increasing. Famine and starvation grow as more and more of the earth is owned by fewer and fewer people. Fear and mistrust are rising on every hand. Families are breaking up, isolation increases, generation gaps widen, children are abandoned, abused, neglected. People try to escape through drugs or actual suicide. The courts and prisons cannot keep up with the rising rate of crime, which is itself becoming more and more violent. Terrorism is the political mode of the times, between nations, races, religions, and political factions. Terror stalks the streets of the major cities of the civilized world. Governmental intelligence agencies plot assassinations and the overthrow of governments. Multinational industrial cartels squeeze the last life's blood out of the earth and her tribal and peasant peoples, while the military complex fingers its triggers and demands more sophisticated weapons of destruction.

You don't have to be a scientist or a visionary to see where all of this must inevitably lead. And no one who has the public's attention, no political leader, no voice of authority and respect, has put forward any workable solution to all this. The solutions offered are only more of the same.

Under these conditions I do not find it strange that there is such apathy and frustration, such hopelessness and barely suppressed anger among people today. I do not find it surprising that young people turn to drugs or cults or the immediate thrills of sensual pleasures or to amassing wealth and courting fame. It is hard to rally folks to a good cause these days. What cause can mean anything with the numbing catastrophes that are revealed relentlessly in the news media every day of our lives?

And yet when I speak to you here and now, whenever and wherever I speak, at ceremonies, gatherings, on radio and television, the message I bring is one of hope. The message I bear, from prophecy, vision, and instruction by the traditions of my elders, is that it is not too late for those who listen and heed.

Humankind has created all of the problems which it now faces, and humankind can solve them, if we but will. The same genius that has created weapons of incredible destruction and has probed beyond the earth to the very stars could certainly find a way to bring the peoples of earth together for their own survival. But it is as though we were in a burning house and all the people in it, instead of trying to put out the fire, were just redecorating their rooms and even robbing each other to do it.

There is no doubt in my mind that millions of people will not be able to survive the holocaust that we are even now preparing for ourselves. There is also no doubt in my mind that anyone can still find the Sacred Path of the Creator, and that each of us who does has the power to create with others a society of harmony and joy, wiser and stronger for the lessons of this age of terror and confusion.

It is hard, in a world that already has so much suffering in it, to think that it will soon be worse beyond our imagining. But because it is hard, we should not refuse to see it, to look at it, think about it, and to take action in our lives.

People speak of political problems, economic problems, sociological problems, psychological problems, and everyone has a pet theory of how to solve his or her own pet problems. Those are just bandages on the sores of a diseased body. A deeper remedy must be found for the inner cause of the disease. The disease is caused by oppressive and hurtful social systems. We do not see the fundamentally oppressive nature of these systems because all of society teaches and fosters basic philosophical and spiritual errors.

A t the deepest level the disease is spiritual. Spirituality as I conceive it is simply the relationship of all things in the universe. Instead of thinking only of ourselves, we must consider our families, our children, our unborn generations, our planet and all the beings who share it with us, as well as the star–beings throughout the cosmos, and the connections among all of these.

Where it must all begin is with trust. Unless we trust that the Creation is good, that it works, that we are good, and that we can learn to live in a good way in this Creation, we give ourselves over to force or to despair. When we do not trust, we resort to force for protection, to police and armies, and we set up a counterforce. But once we have this trust, we need only to discover the way that Creation works, find the path and follow it. It is the way of harmony, the way of cooperation with natural law. Fortunately, we have many guides who have followed that path before us and many who are following it now. And we have the guide of the heart within us.

There is an old native saying that every step we take upon the Earth Mother should be as a prayer. Now, a prayer is just a way of becoming really conscious, really tuning in to all the relationships of everything in existence. To make every step a prayer is simply to be totally conscious in every act we do. Most of us spend most of our waking hours half asleep, only dimly aware of our feelings, to say nothing of what is going on in the world and of the connections between things.

Whatever we do has a meaning and an effect. We can ask ourselves, if I am really conscious, what effect will this action have upon Creation? How will it affect me, affect my family and my community? How will it affect the planet? How will it affect the future and the generations to come?

Our elders have passed down to us a guide for doing this. Our people call this the Original Instructions. Let us consider those instructions next. Let us begin to retrace our steps and find the Sacred Path again. As we go, let us walk in a sacred manner by letting each step be as a prayer. In this way we will find the Path of Beauty, the Path of the Heart, and return to Creation once more.

Chapter Four

The Original Instructions

Take the magic feather with me now, and let us soar across this shining bay.

Below are the many small bays of my Pokonoket country. Easterly we cross widening Buzzard's Bay separating Pokonoket from Cape Cod, home of our Mashpee Tribe. A string of little sandy islands with green hills and a few woods spills off in a line from the bottom of the cape southwards. Just beyond is the island of Nope, known today as Martha's Vineyard, with its satellite isle of Noman's Land.

The eastern end of Nope is the almost–island of Chappaquiddick, once the home of a tribe by that name. In the north center is the little community of Christiantown, where Nope natives were first converted. Eventually Nope's native people, the Chappaquiddick, the Katama, the Capowack, and the Christiantown people, were forced back by the encroaching European settlements, the remnants joining the people of Aquinnah at the far western end of the island.

Aquinnah is the place of the bright colors. On its northern head are cliffs of colored clay that are constantly changing as they are washed by the rains and the tides. The town today is known as Gay Head, and it is still essentially an Indian town, though not so much as when I was a boy. Richer European Americans have been buying up the land constantly, and the price of our land there is now way out of the range of our people.

The natives here are good people, simple people, living close to the earth and sea. Much of their livelihood comes from the sea, most of the rest from the tourists that come to see the cliffs and the Indians. I have been visiting here since I was a boy, and in those days children could run free all over Gay Head, for there were only our people there. Today there are fences and "No Trespassing" signs everywhere. Jacqueline Onassis has bought a large piece of land here. I hope her intention is to preserve and care for it, but I wish that she would meet with our people there so that they could know her heart, and so she could learn more about this very special and sacred land.

As I say, these are good people, kind and generous, proud and independent, islanders for thousands of years. They are not my band, but I am proud they are of my Wampanoag Nation and that we are relatives and good friends.

O ur stories say that at one time Maushop slept on the curve of Cape Cod. He could change his size at will, it seems, for in some stories he is more gigantic than in others. When he woke he found his moccasins full of sand and hurled the sand from each of them into the sound, and the sand became the islands of Nope and Nantucket. Later, when he discovered Nope, he decided to live there, and with a huge iceberg as a shovel, he gouged out the sound and poured the sand and clay on Nope to enlarge it. What dribbled from the shovel became the Elizabeth Islands, Noman's Land, and the dangerous underwater reef known as the Devil's Bridge.

The name Devil's Bridge came from the Europeans who heard this story. To them any deity not of their own Christian mythology was diabolic, and they taught our people that Maushop was the Devil. The people of Aquinnah have never believed that, but the name "Devil's Hole" likewise remains to identify where Maushop slept just below the cliffs. Today most people do not know that the Devil's Hole refers to Maushop.

At the western end of Nope, Maushop piled the clay high into cliffs of four sacred colors, yellow, red, black and white, the colors of the four directions and the four seasons. Yellow is the color of the day and of the east whence comes the day, the color of the spring; red is the color of the south, of blood, of life, and the summer when things grow; black is the color of night and of the west where the day ends, and of autumn; white is the color of winter, of snow and clouds and the purifying winds of the north. There are other native nations who have these same sacred colors, but not always in the same sequence. For the Lakota, the east and south are opposite to our way. I give the colors as my grandfather taught them to me.

Maushop took the clay in four colors and made four races of human beings to populate the earth. He mixed them in shades of brown, some with more red or white, more black or yellow. This was the gift of the body. Then he gave the gift of the mind, to make tools for hunting and fishing and gardening and shelter and clothing and preparing food, and for music. After that he gave the gift of the heart, so that human beings could know Beauty and Joy and Love. Finally he asked the Creation to give some of its Kishtannit, or Big Spirit, for these human beings to make them live. Then Maushop taught the human beings what they needed to know in order to survive and add their music to the great Song of Creation.

Those teachings are the Original Instructions. Most people who have an ancient oral tradition speak of such instructions, or the instructions are implicit in the tales and legends of the people. These instructions are very similar throughout North America. When our nations gather for intertribal ceremonies and spiritual conferences we learn how close our traditional concepts are, no matter what different languages and customs we have.

It is this concept of Original Instructions that most profoundly distinguishes native spiritual belief from all the man-made religions of the world. The Original Instructions are not ideas. They are reality. They are actually Natural Law, the Way Things Are — the operational manual for a working Creation. They cannot totally be explained in words. They must be experienced. Native people refer to the Original Instructions often in speech and prayer, but rarely attempt to say exactly what they are. They are not like the Ten Commandments carved in stone by a stern authority figure. We have no scriptures, no sacred books to be studied and argued over. The Original Instructions are not of the mind. They are of the spirit, the essence of Creation. Other creatures follow them instinctively. They are communicated to humankind through the heart, through feelings of beauty and love. We observe nature, we tune in to the spirits and feel the Creator's law all around us, silent, mysterious and immutable.

S tand with me now here on the cliffs of Aquinnah. There is no one else here, for it is still early, the sun has just emerged from the ocean to the east. There used to be a custom that young couples wishing to be married would spend the night together and then stand here, hand in hand, to greet the rising sun and pledge their lives together for the new days to come, and for the children with which Kiehtan Kishtannit might bless them. They needed no laws, religious or secular, to know what was right. Their hearts together knew the Path of Beauty, the Original Instructions.

Watch the seagulls dip and glide, following their Original Instructions. The Instructions teach the maple tree how to bring forth its sap just before spring, and we have ceremonies at that time to honor the maple. They teach the birch to make paper bark, and our people honor the birch as a very special and sacred tree. They instruct the strawberry to be the first fruit to appear in spring, and we have ceremonies to honor that occurrence, as well as for the green corn and the cranberry as they follow their instructions in their own seasons. The Instructions show the blueberry, the blackberry, and beech plum how to make their own individual fruits. So it is that an oak tree always grows acorns and not apples. So it is that the ducks and the geese fly south in the winter, but the crow and the blue jay never follow them because they have different Instructions.

Maushop taught the human beings to be glad and to thank all of our relatives for their contribution to Creation. Once, when people forgot to thank Nepaushet Kesuckquand, Grandfather Sun, he went away, and the world was cold and dark until Maushop caught him in a great net and told him that the people would never take that powerful spirit for granted again. And so at the winter solstice we thank the sun for remembering his Original Instructions and stopping his annual journey to distant lands to begin his return for the life of all that grows where we live. At other times we may thank other relatives on the earth — the beans, the squash, the cranberry, the snake, the deer, the beaver, the herring, the salmon, the eagle, the wild goose, the rain, the thunders, the rainbow, Grandmother Moon, the star people, and all things in the universe, known and unknown. All of these beings follow their Original Instructions. It is only humankind that is confused and in conflict, destroying the precious balance that holds together the forces of Creation.

When you are a child your father may give you a knife and say, "I want you to know this thing about knives: if you use them this way they are safe, but if you use them that way you may cut yourself. The knife is not good or evil, that is just the way knives are." That is how the world is.

When we do not follow the Original Instructions we will feel the effects. When we clear-cut the forests and plow up the prairies and strip-mine the hills we create erosion and lose our soil. The loss of topsoil is a major catastrophe in civilized countries, and the loss of water in the water tables below the surface is the beginning of another catastrophe. When we manufacture more and more things we create more and more garbage and pollution and cancer. A hundred years ago cancer was a rare disease, and in many non-industrial areas it is still unknown. The densest industrial areas, such as New Jersey, are the areas of highest cancer rates among the general public. Considering that some radioactive waste has destructive power for hundreds of thousands of years and that we are dumping this poison in our Mother Earth for our unborn generations to have to deal with, we are certainly flouting our Original Instructions to our peril.

T he people on this continent at one time tried to live their lives according to these Original Instructions. They did not always succeed. They were human beings and were not perfect, but growing and learning, like the rest of us. But their lives were structured around these Original Instructions: individual consciousness, family life, social organizations, educational and political and spiritual ways were all in harmony. Despite the frightening tales of the invaders, most of the over five hundred nations of this continent were among the most pacific people that ever inhabited the earth. Here in the Northeast our people created federations of peace that were in place when Alexander was trying to enslave Asia for the Greeks. The Houdinosonie to the west of us created the first United Nations in the world and a peace that has lasted among them for a thousand years. But the Great Law of Peace was not written down. It was kept in the hearts of the People of the Longhouse, so that the spirit, which was attuned to the spirit of Creation, would never be lost.

The first people were in harmony with themselves and all Creation because theirs was not written law. There were no Ten Commandments to be broken, no statutes for police to enforce and lawyers to find loopholes in. An ancient Chinese sage once said, "Where there is no law, there will be no criminals." Human laws create criminals, because they create opposition — they are based on fear and not love. The more laws, the lower the level of trust, and human community functions best on trust. Natural Law enforces itself, there are no loopholes in it. Four hundred years ago on this continent there was no need for a legal profession, and there was no such thing as a criminal profession.

No one lived by hurting others. The Original Instructions are to be found in no book for the scholars to dispute. They are in our hearts, all the time. We all know what is right. You know what is right. You know when you are doing wrong. And when people point out to someone that he has made a mistake and hurt someone, if they are not condemning but helpful, that person will do anything he can to repay the hurt he has caused in order to feel good about himself again.

There is no cruelty in the wilderness, in nature, without human beings. Animals are never cruel. They do not act out of spite or revenge. They do not carry anger or fear beyond the appropriate moment. Only human beings think and understand with their minds that they must die. But with this understanding comes the knowledge of the Original Instructions. For we are the only beings on this earth that can feel and know Beauty in our hearts. When through our acts we create ugliness and imbalance and bad feelings we know this is not the Way of Creation. When we create Beauty and Joy and Love we feel good. Our hearts tell us when we are in harmony and in good balance.

There is a story that First Man asked Maushop what he should do, and Maushop told him his grandmother would know. But First Man had to figure out how to make a boat of logs so he could cross the river, because his grandmother's lodge was on the other side. When he asked his grandmother what he should do, she said, "You have just had your first lesson. Your heart told you to come and speak to me, and your mind showed you how to cross the river. Always use your mind to show you how to follow the direction of your heart, but never the other way around. Your mind can learn, and it knows what it learns, but only the heart knows love and beauty, and they are Creator's guides."

Let us sit here for a while on the cliffs of Aquinnah in silence. Breathe with the wind. This is one of the few places where you can watch the sun arise from the sea to the east, across Nantucket Sound, and watch it descend, as it is now, beyond the islands and Buzzard's Bay to the west. The land grows dim, darkening, but the sea is pale and rosy, holding the last light of the sky. The last tourists have left in the last tour buses, and lights begin to go on in the little houses. Sea gulls wheel above the grass here on the cliffs and hang motionless in the light breeze, dipping down to the smooth sound and the beach below. Life proceeds in its circles everywhere: the circling birds on the winds, the circling fish below the waters, the grass, the scrub oak and piney woods, the beach plums and cranberry bogs, in the streams and ponds. Life. Germinating, growing, feeding, reproducing, giving its life and body back to the circle of Creation again. All following their Original Instructions without thought or choice. But we, sitting here contemplating all this, we are different. We human beings have different instructions.

Creator has given to human beings a special mind, one with imagination. That is what allows us to create, and to devise new and individual solutions for each new problem. With that gift comes the instruction that we use it responsibly. We must be custodians and caretakers of this beautiful Creation and of all life, of all our relatives, human and non–human. That is why we have also been given the special gifts of Love and the senses of Joy and Beauty to guide us in using the gift of choice.

The way that has been given to us to comprehend and follow our Original Instructions is that of the Sacred Circle. That is what we will consider in our next discussion.

Chapter Five

The Sacred Circle

Today let us start from the water. That is where life begins.

First were the stars, runs the ancient tale of Creation, and then the water. The fire and wind spirits were dancing in a Universe of myriad lights, and below them was the still black depths of water, womb of the earth and of her children.

We are a water people, never far from the source of life. For ten thousand years the People of the Morning Light have lived along these bays and on these islands. Before that, our legends tell us, our ancestors crossed the great Turtle Island from the southwest; before that they lived inside a mountain, in the earth; before that they crossed the sea from exploding islands; and before that they lived down under the waters of the great ocean, our ancient grandmother. Our people are one with the spirits of the waters. So this is a good place for our beginning today.

In this quiet grove the bodies of my ancestors have become earth again. Their spirits, our old ones tell us, departed upon the Star Path long ago, guided by Sowunishen, the southwest wind, to the Land of Souls. But the thoughts they have thought have form and remain always. You can hear them in the sighing song of the breeze blowing through the leaves of this place.

Let us take a small boat and row across this little lake we see before us. When I look over into the dark waters lapping the side of the boat, I see the rays of the sun turn black and disappear below us. I can see a dark emanation from the depths of the lake, like dark rays reaching upward from a mysterious source far below. Legends say that many, many years ago a young woman by the name of Scargo wanted a little pond in which to keep some fresh-water fish she had been given as a present. She was well-beloved by her father the chief and by all the young men of the village. It is said that they dug this lake for her with sea clamshells (which in those days were very much larger than they are now). This is Scargo Lake, and Scargo Hill rising yonder from its shores is said to be made of the earth dug by the warriors to make the lake.

The waters look, sound, feel, taste, and smell the same as when I rowed and fished and swam here as a young boy. Looking into that dark mirror I see my jagged old face soften and grow small and smooth, and it is that young boy who was myself that looks back at me out of the depths of time.

For a moment, I can almost believe that all those new houses will not be there when I look back at the hill, that my grandfather will be with me in the boat, and that we will climb the hill and pick blueberries together again.

Well, come then, let us climb. It's a good, steep climb from the lake shore, but it's worth it. When we finally struggle out of the woods at the summit we'll see the lake below us, carved from the earth in the shape of a fish, and beyond is the shining expanse of Cape Cod Bay reaching north to the sea.

There is an old stone tower here. We mount the circular wooden stairs within to the top. The tower is a cylinder of irregular rocks, rather squat, fatter at the bottom, jutting stolidly into the sky from the crest of the hill, glowering above the tangle of trees. It is a memorial, built like many ancient towers throughout Europe and the British Isles. I have seen one very like it built by the ancient Indian peoples above the Grand Canyon in Arizona. There were spiritual reasons for such structures to be circular in construction.

It is the circle that I want to talk about today.

People who live very close to the earth and the natural order of things are very simple and very real. Dreams are real to these people. Apparitions and visions, which

52

more sophisticated people say are "only in our minds," are real to them. The original people of Turtle Island embrace the essential spiritual and mysterious nature of the universe. Things are as they are. Whatever is, certainly is.

Even though the Original Instructions are not written out in some book or scroll of the law, we can perceive them at work through the observation of nature and by the experience of the people over the continuum of time, transmitted to each generation by tribal lore, ceremony, song and story. This is how we are one in a circle of time with our ancestors and with the unborn generations to come.

Thus the Original Instructions suggest to us not only the reality, the is-ness, of all experience and all things, but also their relatedness. All is one circle. We feel a kinship with everything. Animals, plants, stones, mountains, rainbows and stars are all to be addressed as relatives. Even those things which appear strange or frightening in lore or experience have some history, if we can discern it, which connects them in some unknown way to the circle. They have a necessary place.

This is why we think and live in a realm of circles. We see circles in all of nature. We gather together in a circle, we think of our communities as circles, of the races of humankind as a circle. The physical structure of the cosmos, from the smallest particle to the very walls of the universe, is a circle. And all these circles are part of one Great Circle of Existence.

It is important to keep the connection of all these circles to the Great Circle. Sometimes we feel lost. We feel separate. This is an illusion, a sickness. This is one of Matahdou's poisons — the poison to the spirit. Being alone, being separate, this is all illusion. We reinforce that illusion by cutting ourselves off from each other, from the earth and nature, from our very selves.

At one time we did not feel so separate. We lived in harmony with Creation and could communicate with many other spirits. As long as human beings lived in a sacred way they kept that harmony. But when at some point a few people began to forsake the ancient instructions, the illusion of separation began. This illusion is like a demon, for when people believe in it, it becomes real. When we feel separate from the earth then we can own it, conquer it, despoil it, ravage it. When we feel separate from each other we create envy, jealousy, greed, malice, crime, and war. When we feel separate we create the battle of Good and Evil. Evil is only separateness — and separateness is only an illusion.

Strange, isn't it, that this illusion should make us so sick, sick to the point of destroying the whole planet and all our history. Believing the illusion, we have made it real.

This separation begins early, and we have institutionalized it, to insure its power right from the start of our lives. In our modern society, babies are separated from their mothers by strangers at birth and put in cribs, in separate rooms, fed from bottles on a schedule of someone else's convenience, sent away from the family to school while one or more of the parents goes somewhere else to work. The grandparents, aunts, uncles and cousins live somewhere else. The people next door belong to different churches and clubs. The people on the next block, perhaps even in the next apartment, are unknown to us. The streets are paved, the playgrounds are artificial, our food comes from a shopping plaza, as does our clothing and furniture. Our entertainment is created by people far away whom we don't know. Our houses are built by anonymous strangers. We have little sense of family, less of community, and practically no connections with the earth and her natural processes. This whole culture, in its education and art, its philosophy, history, politics and economics, teaches and reinforces the illusion of our separateness from the Creation.

Look down again at the earth below us. There is that little town, smaller, prettier, slower and wealthier than most American communities. The town is over two hundred years old, yet only a few of the families that comprised this town when I was a boy, five decades ago, are still here. That little, wooded area encompassed by an iron rail fence, where we began our journey today across the lake, was the burial ground of the Nobscusset people who inhabited this place for thousands of years. Generation after generation, born close to the earth, living close to earth and sea, were buried in that same earth. Not in this burial ground. Those earlier people were laid to rest close to their own homes, but when the European people began to take over the land of this town, they set aside this plot and told the surviving Nobscussets to re–bury their ancestors here if they wanted to secure their remains. Thousands of years of that culture sleep recondite in that quiet grove by the lake, while the town that supplanted it shifts and changes and refuses to root and grow in this soil.

With a little imagination we can see the world below us as it looked four hundred years ago, before Champlain and Gosnold and the Pilgrims probed these shores. You would not have been able to locate the villages as easily then, even from this vantage point. The houses were small, of natural wood, bark and grasses, blending into the environment. Only the little lines of smoke from fires would indicate areas where human beings lived. There were no highways, no cars or trucks, no stores, no factories, no fences, no electric wires, no flashing lights, no roaring engines, no horns, whistles, explosions. Instead there was the stillness and slowness of ancient processes, the sounds of the wind, the waves along the beach, the waterfalls, the birds, the rustle of little animals among the leaves. In all this weaving of many dances and many songs, human beings moved gently with praise and thanksgiving for the wealth and beauty of this vast circle of Creation.

When the invaders came they had no eyes or ears for this beauty. Once they had established their base and were secure they began to force the natives from their homes and villages and to make them submit to their alien laws. The Europeans felt that the indigenous people were both ignorant and vile — less than human — and therefore could only benefit by submitting to Christian law and religion.

It is true the natives did not know the ways of these conquerors, but they knew one essential thing that the Europeans had long forgotten. They knew the Original Instructions. They knew how to live as a tribe in harmony with Creation. They lived at peace with their neighbors, revered the earth, and had respect for all creatures.

I know this is not the impression you have learned of Indian people in your history books. Remember that those books were written by people who had a lot of explaining to do about their treatment of these other human beings, treatment that does not at all agree with the teachings of their own religion. In order to justify "civilization," the "savage" had to be created. So a picture was painted of a vicious, dirty, crafty, traitorous, unpredictable, violent and terrifying race. Nightmare stories to scare naughty children, pictures of frontier settlements in flames, of encircled wagon trains, of women screaming at the sight of painted warriors are all part of our culture today. Even now little children often shrink from me in real fear, while five–year olds ask more boldly if I kill people and demand to see my tomahawk.

How far from the reality of Indian people this is! Columbus found the natives "artless and generous with what they have, to such a degree as no one would believe but him who had seen it." Traditional people today are the same as he reported them: "Of anything they have, if it be asked for, they never say no, but do rather invite the person to accept it, and show as much lovingness as though they would give their hearts."

An Englishman at Roanoke found the natives "most gentle, loving and faithful, void of all guile and treason, and such as live after the manner of the golden age." Everywhere the early explorers and settlers were met by the natives with kindness and hospitality, until, too late, the inhabitants discovered the real motives of these invaders. Even today, should you visit an Indian family, you would experience that same hospitality, and, like the artist George Catlin who traveled extensively among the Indians, you would "share, with a hearty welcome, the best that his wigwam affords for the appetite, which is always set out to a stranger the next moment after he enters." Catlin, who knew the Plains Indian better than the authors of histories, says, "The reader . . . should forget many theories he has read in the books of Indian barbarities, of wanton butcheries and murders; and divest himself, as far as possible, of the deadly prejudices which he has carried from his childhood. . . ."

Those European settlers of four hundred years ago had been victims of several millennia of oppression, imperialism, colonialism, tyranny, religious bigotry and class hatred. Having suffered from a history of warfare and cruelty, of greed and slavery, they tried to escape to America. If they could have also escaped their conditioning and their fears, they might have been able to notice some very important features of this Turtle Island four hundred years ago, features that are not much considered even today.

If you stood here four hundred years ago you would see no public buildings anywhere. All the needs of the community would be cared for within the circle of that tribe. One very big difference is that you would not be able to find any place of constraint for human beings. We remarked in our last talk that our people had no written laws, no lawyers, no courts, no judges, no legal profession at all. There were also no prisons on Turtle Island. That is quite amazing when you consider that today governments cannot build enough prisons, and all the prisons and the courts are overcrowded. But then there were no jails, no reform schools, no police. There was no criminal class: no professional burglars, robbers, highwaymen, pickpockets, kidnappers, extortionists, forgers, embezzlers, swindlers, racketeers — and no alcohol or drug abuse. Of course there were some who made human mistakes occasionally. Human folly exists in the best of societies. But there was not such a thing as a whole class

56

of people who excluded themselves from the circle of society, an "underworld" society that lived by taking advantage of honest people.

George Catlin wrote in the early nineteenth century: "There is no law in their land to punish a man for theft — that the commandments have never been divulged amongst them; nor can any human retribution fall upon the head of a thief, save the disgrace which attaches as a stigma to his character, in the eyes of his people about him." Disgrace! Ostracized! How powerful is that circle! "And thus in these little communities, strange as it may seem, in the absence of all systems of jurisprudence, I have often beheld peace and happiness and quiet, reigning supreme, for which even kings and emperors might envy them. I have seen rights and virtue protected, and wrongs redressed; and I have seen conjugal, filial and paternal affection in the simplicity and contentedness of nature."

Sometimes people, when they hear me say this, say, "Oh, well, there just weren't so many people here then." I will admit that scale does have a lot to do with the human treatment of human beings. People suffer so much stress in the great mass that they tend not to see and treat each other as human beings. However, there were a lot more people here than most people seem to realize. There were more than thirty thousand people in my small nation. At the same time most of the communities in Europe also were not large, but they were full of laws and criminal activity.

If the early Christian settlers had not been so blinded by their own history and conditioning, they might have seen that the inhabitants of the new world had achieved something their old world had not been able to do. Here was a society motivated by love, and by trust in the order and rightness of the universe. It was motivated by trust because the people remained close to the natural processes of life. They believed there was a purpose for all the things in Creation, and that their work was not to conquer or dominate but to understand and nurture, to appreciate and enjoy. It was motivated by love, too, because the basic unit of society was not the individual but the family. They found that the family was best served by banding with other families in the mutual support system of a tribe, and that the individual was best served by giving to each equal respect and freedom. There was no coercion. Children were taught by example, not by punishment. There were no constraints, save the desire of each person to be thought well of within the tribe. All lived by natural law which all understood. That is why there were never any prisons on Turtle Island. That is also why there were no orphanages, old people's homes, poor farms, or asylums; no welfare, food stamps, social security, labor unions or organizations were necessary to protect the rights of minorities or children or animals or the environment.

Does it seem impossible to you that the world should ever be able to return itself to such a condition of trust and love again? If human beings have created the society which requires all these constraints and supports, laws and taxes, and if human beings also once constructed a society which did not need these things, haven't human beings enough intelligence to figure out how to get back to a society based on trust and love? I, of course, think we do. That's why I'm talking about it with you. There are many people who are trying to live lives that are different from those of this constraining society, and many of them are succeeding in creating their own tribal societies. Later I will tell you about some of these people, as their experience may serve not only as an inspiration, but as a guide to others.

But before we talk about what we can do or about what others are doing, it might be good to look some more at the experience and inherited wisdom of our old tribal ways. For hundreds of thousands of years, for most of human existence, humankind has lived tribally. Only in recent times, in this modern phenomenon of a civilization that is only a few millennia old in its oldest places, have tribal ways and knowledge been forsaken. From our tribal ancestors we inherit, in the buried recesses of our minds, a dim memory of living within the circle. Civilization, in that scale of time, is still very new. It is certainly appropriate to consider changing its forms in ways that will nourish rather than inhibit our humanity.

Today in America, more and more people long for that circle, for a family, a tribe, a world they have never known. But, not having been raised in such a world, they do not know how to create it. They cannot stay in one place, cannot live for any length of time with their parents, cannot keep their families together. They keep changing partners and shuffling their children around amongst them. They try experiments in group living and in "going back to the land," which most often do not work out for them because they do not and never did understand the basic requirements of tribal living.

It is not hopeless. It is still possible to learn from those who keep the ancient ways and wisdom.

The basic elements of tribal life are spiritual. To understand the tribe you must first know that Creation is a circle made of circles. You must know that humankind is a circle made of all the circles of all the nations, the nation a circle of the circles of its tribes, and the tribe a circle of the circles of its families. Our circles connect through time, so that we not only have a place in the family and the tribe, but also in the spiral that connects our ancestors with the unborn generations to come.

The deepest, strongest, best feelings of my life are the ones I get when I regard my children. Watching them learn, play, hurt, laugh, or just sleep, I am overwhelmed by the deepest awe. At that moment I know my Original Instructions clearly. I hear the Creator whisper in my ear to do my utmost for these, and teach them to do the same for their children, and that where all this love and all this learning is going is what the Creation is all about. Our children are the growing edge of the conscious evolution of life on this planet.

My Original Instructions tell me to be a tribal being, since it is in the warm, loving, accepting, appreciating environment of the tribe that my children are going to flourish best. Whether I am biologically a parent or not, in the tribe I am a parent of all the children. To the extent that I forget or lose that feeling, that nourishing and caring for the growth of all our little ones, to that extent exactly the work of my life will lose contact with the Sacred Path that is the way of Creation.

Do you see how it all fits together? The Original Instructions are the Circle. I am a circle, but not isolated, not separate. I join with a woman, and we have children. Now our individual circles are together in another circle — the family — which includes the grandparents and uncles and aunts and cousins — and these join in another circle — the tribe. The tribe draws its circle upon the Earth Mother and says so much will we protect and care for, and she will provide for us. Then our tribal circle looks to the neighboring tribes and comes to one mind with them to protect and care for that region of the earth. And now in our modern era of technology we can extend this all around the planet.

But the basic circle is still the tribe: the largest number of people that can live in the intimate sharing of the resources of our immediate environment. When we get beyond that we create abstractions, states, governments, corporations. We have the illusion that we control these creations, but they are monsters with lives of their own, and soon they have usurped all our power. We are powerless within our own institutions.

Yet the Original Instructions are there still. They are still in our blood, in our genes, in our heritage. We fall in love. We conceive children. We long for the security of our tribe, our own people, our own sacred land. Our society is crumbling all around us, and still in our ears we can hear, if we but listen, the voice of the Creator whispering in the night, telling us to hold our loved ones tight, to keep our families together, to embrace our neighbors, to share the beauty and the bounty of the earth in one sacred circle.

Chapter Six

A Society of Love

We are on a mountain top. It is late in the afternoon of an early spring day. The sky holds no clouds, and the brisk wind is beginning to subside as the sun moves closer to the western horizon. The mountain's name is Wachusett. We climbed to the top in only a few hours because it is a very small mountain. It is small because it is very, very old, far older than the great peaks of the West, or of South America or Asia. When it was a young mountain it was five miles high, now it is a half mile above the sea. It has seen much, and it is a very sacred place.

Mountains have a very special power. Each one has its own spirit, its own quality, its own personality. Climbing one and staying quietly alone upon it, you get to know a mountain. If you open yourself it will speak to you. The size of the mountain has nothing to do with its power or its wisdom.

This mountain has known ten thousand years of our people. When our ancestors migrated here it was already very ancient. The millennia since then have been a mere wink in the life of this old mountain. In the old days a person might make a pilgrimage to this sacred mountain and camp alone upon it to seek a vision or the answer to a difficult problem.

It was here that Metacomet held a great council of many tribes and nations, hoping to unite all our people in driving

the perfidious English invaders from our shores. I feel his
presence here sometimes. I stand here and imagine all the
people gathered across this mountaintop from all the lands
down below, listening in respectful silence to the great
sachem's words. As they looked out they could see the
English presence moving inexorably out across their land
and, more crucially, the English law and customs dominating the earth and their own people more and more. In
fifty-five years the English had gone from welcomed friends
to conquerors. The time had come to resist. But even now it
was too late. Unfortunately for his plan, so many of our
villages, already decimated by European diseases, had been
so infected with Christianity that true unity was impossible.
The last brave resistance of our people was defeated in
1676. The English conquest was complete.

Below us where we now see towns and the cities of
Fitchburg, Leominster, and Worcester, were once the little
villages of the Nipmuc people amid the ancient forests. To
the north rises the beautiful solitary peak of Monadnock,
also a very ancient and very holy mountain. Farther north,
beyond our sight is the land of the Pennacook people and
the White Mountains. East of them is K'tahdin, a mountain
sacred to the Wabanaki, where the Penobscot River rises.

A mountaintop is a good place for seeing the whole of
things. Here one can see the four directions of the world,
the whole circle of the horizon and the whole of the sky. It
is a good place to put what we have been discussing into a
single vision so we can see it whole.

We have spoken of the need for trust, particularly the
need to trust in the Way of Creation. We have dis-
cussed the need to trust our ability to follow our vision and
find our way on the Path of the Heart, making every step a
conscious one, a prayer.

We have spoken of the Original Instructions, and of each
of us carrying these instructions which we may know if we
seek them. Foremost among these instructions, according to
our old ones, is respect and care for our Sacred Mother the
Earth and respect and care for all of our relatives who share
this mother with us.

We have spoken of the sacred circle. We have seen that
to carry out our instructions human beings must come
together in a circle with a common agreement to care for the
part of the Earth Mother which shelters and sustains us, to
care for each other and for all other beings that share
that land with us. We have called this kind of social organi-

zation, tribal.

Indigenous peoples of North America, and many other tribal peoples around the world, had a relationship of custodial responsibility to the plants, the animal life, the waters and soil of the land, the particular valley or watershed or area which supported them. We have seen that the tribal way kept people in harmony with their life support system and with each other for over a million years, but civilization has tended to destroy even the memory of that harmonious relationship.

Most people have a sense of their history which is bounded by what is written. My sense of history is on a much larger scale. Written history is only a few thousand years old, so it is civilization centered. But our people have been here for over a million years. In that frame civilization is a short-term experiment that hasn't quite worked out. Maybe if we take a longer view we can still fix it up.

Look again at the earth spread below us, the little houses, the towns, the roads, the cities, the fields and woodlands, the valleys, streams and hills. This earth has been here for billions of years, and life has existed on it for nearly that long. For all those billions of years no living being owned or dominated this land. The earth and all her creatures thrived. Each took from the land only what it needed for survival. For over a million years human beings lived on the earth without owning or dominating it, until only a few thousand years ago, when the concept of ownership began to spread through Asia, northwestern Africa and southwestern Europe. Then boundaries, armies, cities, states and empires came into being.

But the land that we see below us now was not owned by any person until a little over three hundred years ago when English settlers began to purchase grants from the Massachusetts Bay Colony, which illegally claimed ownership of the territory. For ten thousand years before that our people lived in these valleys and never put up a wall or a fence, never made a survey or recorded a deed, never drew a boundary upon the earth, never conquered or disputed territory, never demanded customs or refused hospitality. For ten thousand years the people lived in harmony with all the creatures that shared this land with them, and for all that time the land, this very land we see below us now, gave its bounty freely. There was more than enough for everyone to have a good life.

Four hundred years ago when a little baby was born in one of the villages of the valleys below us, that baby was assured a place in this land. She or he would share equally the gifts of Mother Earth. She or he would always have many relatives — the immediate family, the tribal band to which he belonged, the animals, the plants, the hills and streams. The child grew up in a friendly world, was welcome and had a place.

Today when a baby is born in one of those hospitals below us there is only a small chance it will have a loving home and a secure place in this world. Only a very small proportion of the parents will be both together and loving. The infant cannot expect the appreciation and support of a tribe, or expect to share freely in the bounty of these fields and woods and streams. These children will not grow up to build their houses, plant their gardens, hunt and fish freely in their lands. If they can't find a job they will have to go on welfare, or into the armed forces. If they are lucky they may spend one-third of their lives working at a dull routine in a pollution-producing factory that also produces shoddy, use-less articles with a planned-in obsolescence to add to the mounting garbage of this world. They will feel powerless to affect decisions regarding the use of the land and resources of their native area. They will be told they don't even have that right, because the land belongs to others. They will settle for just trying to pay the rent, buy the groceries, have a car and a television, get drunk on Saturday night, and not think too much about the oppression and starvation and wars, much less the polluting of their life-support system.

I know it sounds as though I have set up that descrip-tion to show the worst case, but that is the life of most of the people we see filling the buildings and the cars on the highways below us. And these people are typical of the most "advanced" society in the civilized world. This society — based upon ownership — controls and wastes most of the earth's resources, and in so doing creates the oppression, hunger, and violence that are for most of the people below us only another television program.

Yet it is within our power to change all this.

We have said that we need to understand what it means to be human, with the bodies, minds, hearts and spirits we have been given. We have felt the urging of Creation within us to develop and expand our limitless physical, mental, emotional and spiritual capacities. We have said that the very least that is required of us now is to heal the earth and bring peace to the races of humankind.

We see that all the problems that beset human beings

are caused by human beings. But we must trust that human beings are fundamentally and naturally good. We are also fundamentally and naturally intelligent and creative. If we are to heal the earth and each other, we must believe that it is possible. We must be able to dream great dreams of a perfect world and know that we can make these dreams into reality. That is why we are given these visions of earthly paradise, with all beings living in harmony and love.

Everyone has such a vision. Perhaps it is locked deep inside, perhaps ridiculed and hidden. But it is there. I am sure of it. It is part of our Original Instructions. It is the healing, transforming spirit of Creation. To ignore it rather than heed and follow it with all the energy of our bodies, minds, hearts and souls would be the greatest folly and error of our lives.

It is necessary to trust the goodness of human beings. It is necessary to trust our own instincts for good, the Creator Spirit in us. We must understand that all human beings are born good, helpless and trusting. We expect that this is a friendly world and that we will be taken care of. We are born with a boundless capacity for loving, for appreciation of beauty and joy, with great enthusiasm and energy and an intelligence that knows no limit. Have you noticed the energy that a free infant has? Have you seen the fantastic learning power of little babies?

If we are given love and appreciation these capacities will develop naturally. To the extent that we are not loving and joyful and intelligent it is because our experiences in life have blocked this natural development. These growth imped-ing experiences are not the results of our interaction with the animal and plant life, with the earth, moon, sun or stars. Only our experience of other human beings limits us, hurts, twists, retards, deadens us. We do this to our little babies, to each other, systematically, institutionally, from the moment of birth to the moment of death.

As a native person I tend to think in fours. So I think if we are to transform the world and ourselves to Crea-tion's highest vision, we must consider four relationships.

First, we must consider the relationship of human beings to the earth. We must realize that our life–support system is really in jeopardy. We are chopping away at the limb we are sitting on, and we are arguing about whether we should chop faster or slower or if the bough will ever be cut through. We must seek harmony with Creation above all other considerations.

Second, we must consider the relationship of social groups to each other, nation to nation, religion to religion, race to race, gender to gender, generation to generation, class to class, to bring peace without oppression as a minimum for our brief years upon the earth.

Third, we must consider the relationship of the individual to society, to allow the maximum of freedom, creativity and support for each person.

Fourth, we must consider the relationship of individuals with each other, how we can accord each other unconditional love and appreciation from the moment of birth through each hour of living.

Most people are asleep, in a trance. This seems to be the only way to deal with the enormity of the forces around us. Crisis builds on crisis so quickly in the modern world we are numbed, feeling helpless and apathetic in the profusion of problems and horrors around us. We refuse to see them building and increasing, to see how imminent is the final crisis that could render the planet uninhabitable to the human species. We have no understanding of how quickly we are moving. It would be best to be working at the transformation of these relationships with all our energies and abilities all the time.

According to many of the prophecies of our people, the crisis will come in this next generation. The ones who are babies now and the ones being born will inherit a world far more dangerous and deadly than the one that was passed on to us. To halt the destruction and to return to Creation, we will need a generation that has not been made stupid, apathetic, crazy or violent by the oppressive institutions of society.

We need to protect our children from those oppressions from the moment of conception. We need to protect the mothers from an unsafe, unstable environment. We need to provide the most conscious and beautiful birthing transitions for our babies.

We need to protect those babies from the damaging effects of separation and isolation. Civilization takes its children from their mothers, puts them in little bins in the hospital, then in separate cribs, even separate rooms. When they start to crawl they get put in cages.

Later they get sent away to school, to sit at separate desks and do what some representative of society tells them to do, to learn what society demands of them. They learn the ways of society, the ways that are destroying the earth, destroying peace, destroying love. They learn to compete with each other, to fear each other instead of to help and share and cooperate with each other. They learn about boundaries and enemies. They learn chauvinism, racism, sexism and consumerism. They learn that primitive people are ignorant and obsolete, and that it has been the white man's burden to educate them (or eliminate them) in the march of "progress." They learn that nature is hostile, to be conquered, tamed, controlled and exploited by "man." They learn about Daniel Boone and Buffalo Bill but not about Sweet Medicine and Black Elk.

The separation and the lessons are continued by television, that hypnotic, distorting, trivializing brainscrubber. The competition for jobs, security, status, and the threats of inflation, depression and taxation complete the education of a life circumscribed by anxiety and loneliness.

What happened to love in all this?

Our elders tell us that love is the meaning of the circle, the essential instruction of Creation for human beings. Love binds us to the earth and to life. All the prophets and saints and sages of the world have always said that love is the central experience of life. It's what it is all about. Since practically everyone agrees about that, why do we allow ourselves to continue creating social, political, and economic institutions that foster separation, competition and fear, instead of fostering love?

Life is what we all have in common, what we all wish to enhance. Life is the only treasure, a glorious, mysterious gift. The other great gift to human beings is awareness. These two are both very mysterious and very sacred.

There is a familiar saying that God is Love. I understand this to mean that love is the highest good there is. It is in all human beings, even in those where it seems not to reside, having been seemingly frightened or beaten out of existence. I have always found this to be true. I have seen the meanest, coldest, most cruel, unfeeling and deadened souls where love seems to have long died, and I have found its embers there still warm and buried under cold ashes of rage. I always knew it must be there. I would not believe that they or anything else in the universe are not a part of the Spirit/God/Love of Creation.

Love is the awareness of relationship. In the strongest experience of love we feel total awareness, total identification. We are at one with our beloved, one being, existing in one space, one time. The effect is to expand our space beyond all limits and our time towards eternity. In perfect love we feel infinite and timeless. Love of anybody or anything can give us this feeling. When we fall in love with one person, suddenly we start to feel more kindly towards everyone. Our love expands to others. We love the world more. We love ourselves, we love all of Creation. We love life and all that is happening in the universe. It is our home, our family. We love the reason for it, the cause of it, this life, this universe, this wonderful feeling. At the highest ecstasy we are so in love with it all, we are one with Creation. We know that we are awareness. We know that we are love.

L ove. That is what is really happening in the universe. It is there, in all the laws of Creation, as the connection. It fuels the struggle towards self–awareness and awareness of relationship. It is the very essence of life. What is life to a human being without love? Humanity, that species blessed with self–awareness, needs that perception of connectedness we feel as love. From the moment we are born we seek it, this connection to the mystery we call existence. If love is given we learn love. If love is withheld we become disassociated, estranged, confused, then fearful, angry, hurt — finally indifferent, aloof, protected, invulnerable. Yet in our hearts that emptiness aches and yearns and always seeks the connection we call love. And the need to love is even stronger than the need to be loved.

Love is the greatest enhancer of life that there is. Love: that feeling of connectedness, of rightness, of beauty, that ultimate rapture. It can restore health to our bodies and our communities. It can inspire undreamed of creativity.

N ow, if it is true that life is of paramount importance to us and that love is the greatest enhancer of life, the intelligent thing to do would be to create an environment which above all other considerations fosters life and love.

But this is hardly the world which we have built for ourselves and our children. We have created a civilization in which material possessions, power and prestige are held up as standards of achievement and excellence. In a truly loving world we would teach our children by example to share the earth and her bounty equally. We would not seek to dominate but rather to help others grow and find their own powers. We would not wish fame and prestige for ourselves in order to be above others, but would accord recognition, appreciation and honor to all for their different and special attributes. The fruits of our civilization are not only automobiles and television, organ transplants and space probes. They are also interpersonal conflict, paranoia, violence, crime, drug addiction, and war. These are not the fruits of love.

How did this happen? If love is natural to human beings, how did we get to be so separated from each other?

Of course, I wasn't there, but I am sure that however it happened, it was fear that drove us apart. It was fear that first pressed man to dominate the earth and his fellow creatures. I say "man" because women had no part in that domination and were allowed neither power nor ownership. Our early societies, yours as well as mine, were circles, where all were equal and all shared equally. Such a society allows our natural propensity for love to flourish. But when the resources are grabbed up out of fear, then a system of domination must hold that society together. The domination creates more fear, dissension, rebellion, and finally, more domination. So fear creates domination which creates fear and more domination in an endless cycle. Now we have a society which functions on contention. Everything is a battle. Justice is not based upon the truth but upon whoever is clever enough to win in court — usually whoever is rich enough to hire the cleverest advocate. The society solves its issues of state by an adversary system that creates a dissatisfied minority. Poor people don't get good food because the food industry competes to sell them the cheapest chemical comestibles for the greatest profits, while natural healthy foods are more expensive. We have a huge defense budget and mass neurosis over the prospect of nuclear annihilation, which is possible because the fears of nation–states are created out of the same fears that plague us all.

Can this be changed? Can you imagine a society of love? What would it be like? I'll let you think about that now for a while. Because if we start to change it together, I realize it won't be my vision that we create; it will be our vision. In the talks we have together we will look at different aspects of how a society of love, the sacred circle, used to function at its best on this continent. Then we will look at some of the ways people are trying to create a society of love today.

How can we change it? We'll talk more about that later, too. Basically, I think we have to formulate our visions and share them with each other wherever and whenever we can, as often as possible. Those whose visions seem to support each other will join and work together wherever they are.

This is what I have done. When my visions became clear I realized there were not enough people with such a vision where I was, or among the people of my nation. So I began to speak my vision and found others who had similar visions, and we began to create a sacred circle and then found a piece of the earth to care for. Others have been doing this in other places. Now we begin to connect with each other. As we grow, our circles will join to become villages, our villages will join for mutual support within bio-regions. Our conscious reaching out in love and sharing will encompass the earth. But our authority is in our circles, where all are equal.

The most striking thing about the small cooperative community that shares this land where I am now living is the amount of love that exists among these people. We are all of different backgrounds, different nations and races and experiences, and of course we have different ideas about how to do things. There are conflicts of style and taste and interest among us as well. But the love that has grown from putting our lives and energies together is so strong and so healing that it nourishes and sustains all we do.

Now that our own circle is strong and secure and a model to others of a good life — loving, creative, joyful — I travel far into the world, into many nations, talking of the sacred circle and of a society of love. I help create circles where I go and teach others how to create more circles. As these circles survive and become more numerous we will begin the next step of joining these circles into villages. Already, in our little circle of Mettanokit where I live, we are quite self-sufficient. We rely on our own resources and on cooperative interaction with others and have little need for most of the services of government. In a peaceful, egalitarian world we do not need the defense departments of outmoded governments, their welfare, education, labor, revenue and enforcement departments. Our circles becoming villages will give us even more creative opportunities as they become centers of our own cultural expression. Our villages and regions will be able to really concentrate their energies beyond survival, for medicine and research and larger creative projects.

When I travel, telling stories and bringing people together in circles that heal and nourish the lives of others in the great world, I feel the love of each one wherever I am. I know I could settle right down there with that circle of people and build a world on the love we share. But I have my own circle built already, my family, my children are waiting, and I miss them so much. When I come home, I know what will happen. The first time each one sees me, from the baby to the oldest, she or he will light up in a great smile and shout my name and run to hug me and tell me how wonderful it is that I am home again.

In most of the places where I travel I do not see this kind of love in the communities. Now it is becoming even rarer in the homes. When Mother Teresa accepted an award from Harvard University she told the audience that though there may not be naked, starving people lying in the streets of America, that people here are all starving for love. It seems that love is hard to find in most "civilized" areas of the world, rich or poor, urban or suburban. The family values of all nations and races are being destroyed on our mean streets. It is love of consumer goods, of affluence, position, and prestige that is taught by the values of this society.

Yet I could take you to places where I have been in this world where this is not yet so. With our magic feather we could visit small communities and big families where love is still the value that is lived and taught by how they live. These are poor people in goods and in ambition, but rich in the true treasures of life. They are people living in the old ways, close to the earth and their sources of nourishment. They live in the mountains and distant valleys of North, Central and South America, hunting sea mammals in Greenland and reindeer in Scandinavia. They are in areas of every continent, still surviving within the greedy maw of the communist and capitalist worlds. They range the back areas of great Russia, the Indian subcontinent, the hills between Burma and India, the deserts of Africa and Asia, the outlands of Australia, and the island worlds of the Pacific. They are peasants and fisherfolk, craftspeople and healers, migrants and villagers. When we come to their homes there are not eight locks on the door and a peephole or a camera on us. The door is open, the children laugh and gather around us. There is food for us on the table. No matter how little they have, they will share it with us. We see the love in their eyes, and we wonder how long it will be before civilization invades and ends that life forever.

What would our culture be like if it grew from a society of love, where peace, equality, justice and freedom were so established that we no longer even needed words for them? Is not love the one experience of this existence that we should not only welcome but build into the very structure of all our institutions as the primary good and goal?

Many years ago I was attending the annual sun dance of the Arapaho people on the Wind River Reservation of Wyoming. At that time I met, in a house in Lander, a black man from the country of Liberia. He was talking to a friend of mine, and when I caught some of what he was saying I ran to collect some other friends. I told them it seemed important for us to hear this man.

We formed a circle and sat to hear the man's story. He told us some of the history of his country. Liberia was created in the last century by freed slaves from America, although the single real founder was a white American. It was a colony of the United States from 1816 to 1848, when the governor, a free-born octaroon from Virginia, proclaimed an independent republic. During the next seven years the black American immigrants along the coast emulated western ways, including Protestantism and the official English language, while the indigenous native population in the interior maintained the old ways of their tribes. In the 1920's the Firestone Tire and Rubber Corporation obtained a million acres of the country, and American industrialism with its new economic colonialism began to grow. Liberia continues to grow in the U.S. model. The leading citizens are Americo-Liberians, descendants of the American blacks who founded the country. Liberians are prominent in commerce and Europeans in industry. Life on the coast is thoroughly westernized. Monrovia is a typical western city. In the interior of the country, tribal life is disintegrating and the old ways departing.

All this was very distressing to our new friend. Since the American influence and opinion was still paramount in his country, he had come here to get a degree in theology (to gain spiritual credence and avoid being politically suspect). But it was his ambition to begin to counter the forces of both socialism and capitalism and return to the tribalism of his ancestors.

To most people this would seem foolish, romantic atavism, naive, simplistic escapism. In the struggle between the worlds of capitalism and socialism the Third World takes sides or plays off one against the other to get into the game. It is only the Fourth World, the world of native tribal people, that resists the tides of economic growth, industrialism, centralization, institutionalization, statism, legalism, and secularism, all thought to be standards of enlightenment and progress by the rest of the modern world. This is the age of

General Motors, General Electric, General Dynamics, General Telephone, General Foods, General Mills, the age of condominiums, shopping malls, of credit cards and computer warfare. How can any practical person seriously believe we could convert our enormous and complex economic, political, social and religious systems into small cooperative ones?

But our friend had lived in both worlds. He knew the tribal life in its old forms better than any of us, and for him it was the only life worth considering. It was not that he was against technology or modern medical facilities. He could not understand why these could not co-exist in the natural world. He did not see why the jungle had to be laid bare and the people crowded into shanty towns and inner-city slums, with the mass of the country's wealth and political power residing in the hands of one small class of people. He did not see why his people could not manage to have roads and ambulances and fire engines and helicopters without exploiting each other and the environment.

In the tribe, he said, people owned houses but not land. How could a person own land? Are we not all children of the earth? Is the earth not meant for all to share — all creatures of the earth? We all nodded in agreement. It was good to hear this man from another land speak the truths that people have forgotten. Good to know this truth still exists all around the world among people who still remember the old ways.

His tribe had a common garden where all might plant and share the harvest. A person could also grow certain things for himself in a separate garden, and no one else would take from it without asking. But there was always enough, and people were generous. Their needs were simple, and it took very few hours of communal energy to provide a good life for all. Hunters gave part of their kill to families who had none. Everyone was equal, and no one had much more than anyone else. They feasted and sang and danced, they worked together, played games and told stories as people have around the world for a million years and more. They had enough.

Then came the colonizers to teach the ways of civilization. We have been taught to think of "civilization" as a gentling of manners, a restraint of aggression, and a development of arts and ideas. But the history of civilization is one long series of aggressions by very ungentle and unmannerly "civilized" nations against inoffensive primitive peoples, totally heedless of the richness of their culture and spiritual thought.

C ivilization arose in attitudes of superiority, intolerance, and exploitation. The word civilization comes from the Roman word for state. Anyone who lived in the world beyond the Roman state was "uncivilized," just as the world of the Greeks was divided into Greeks and barbarians. Like other civilizations before them, Greek and Roman societies were based upon conquest, subjugation, and the enslavement of other peoples. Civilization and feudalism are inseparable in their origins.

The man who by strength or cunning could control other men and lands could build a bigger house, a palace, a city. He needed an army to secure his position and protect his domain. Whoever lived there was under his protection. That included priests, and so he ordained an official religion which supported him in exchange for official recognition and patronage. The nature of cities is that they attract more and more people, but they are unable to feed such a large population with food grown within the area of the city, so more land and resources must be sought. The cities reach out their tentacles further and further, until they collide with other cities, with which they combine by federation or conquest. Thus cities grow to states, states become empires, empires rise and fall. This is the history of civilization.

The ancient history was mirrored again as civilization came to Liberia. The tribal lands were cut up and allotted, fairly and equally, to each individual of the tribe. But human beings, though they are equal in the sight of Creation, are not alike. Some are quick, some are slow; some are strong, others are not; some like to hunt; some like to plant; some like to build; some like to sing and tell stories. All have different abilities. In a competitive economy some are going to succeed, and others are not. The successful will buy more land, the unsuccessful will be forced to sell their land and seek work for wages from the successful.

"Now," recounted our black friend, "there are things in Liberia there never used to be. There are rich people, and there are starving people. There are social welfare programs and taxes. There is crime. There are police and courts and prisons. There are also big hospitals, but the poor cannot afford to go to them, and most of the people are poor."

Our friend stripped off his shirt and showed us the elaborate tattoo patterns all over his torso.

"This is my diploma," he said proudly. "Wherever I go in the interior people see this and know I am a medicine man. They call on me to heal them, and I must do it, but I can charge no money. They give me a gift — vegetables, a goat, or whatever they can. If they have nothing to give, it is no disgrace. I will still help them, and they will be able to help someone themselves sometime."

We nodded our understanding again. Then we began to speak of how it used to be with our people, in the old times, before the Europeans came. We recalled that at the heart of those ways was the same sense of trust. Then the European Americans in our circle remembered that their ancestors were once too a tribal people. There was this memory in their hearts, along with an emptiness, a longing for the village life where neighbor helped neighbor, where no one wished to be richer or more powerful than others, where all had enough and the sharing was not just of things of the world, but of the mind and the heart, of music and play, of sorrow as well as joy.

We all knew in our hearts that even if it had never been this way in the whole story of the human race, this was the way it should be, the way it must become, for this was the vision that we all, in our most lucid moments, shared in common.

We spoke of our desire to see the world of the tribe bound spiritually to the earth and all life return, and grow even better. We said we were trying to advance this consciousness among ourselves and our people. We said we were trying to learn how to achieve this vision we all shared.

"But you must come to my country!" our friend exclaimed. "You must visit Liberia and tell them that all Americans do not believe in capitalism and federalism. They wouldn't believe me. We have never heard voices like yours in little countries like mine. We only hear the Firestone Company and the Coca Cola Company and the rich tourists. Your dreams could light a sacred fire of hope in many dark, forlorn places."

We stood and brought our circle closer, arms around each other, and fell silent for a long time. We felt the oneness of our common humanity. Then our black friend, our brother from across the other side of the world, spoke again.

"This is the most important thing that we lost when we lost the tribes." He squeezed the shoulders beside him. "This is what we had then. So the only important thing in life was lost to us." His eyes were swollen with unreleased tears.

"What was lost," he said, "was love."

Chapter Seven

The Way
of Beauty

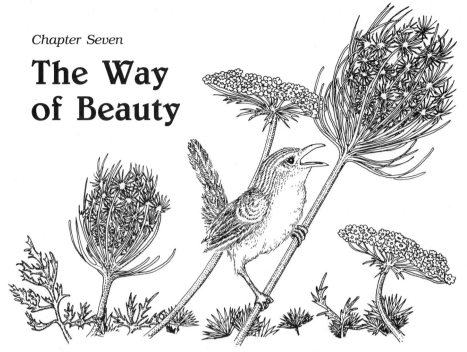

*It is high summer. We are on a green hill. A warm, steady
onshore breeze fondles the leaves of the poplars and strokes
the marsh grass below. Above is a sky of tender blue with
only a few pale clouds low on the eastern horizon. To all
these the deep vibrant blue of the bay flashing in the sun
plays a steady countermelody in the gentle song of summer.
Sitting here quietly I am suffused and absorbed in beauty.*

That sparkling expanse of lively blue water over there is
Turkey Bay. That's the way our ancient people called the
broad reach that separates our people from our neighbors,
the Turkey People. Today it is known by their name, Narragansett Bay.

In these talks, I would like to begin to talk not only
about how it used to be, but also to think about how we
might take the knowledge of the past and blend that with
the best knowledge of today to find better ways for us to live
together. I want to consider together how we might change
this world, this society, this culture, this civilization, into one
that is more human, more consistent with the way of Creation and our Original Instructions.

The place where I sit, this natural seat jutting from the
great rocks of the hillside, was the traditional seat of one of
our greatest supreme sachems, Metacomet, here by his home
village of Montaup. Often he would sit here and look out

upon the same scene that we see before us now. Here, no doubt, he would ponder Creation, his place in it, and his responsibilities to it and to his people, while filling himself with the same beauty that fills us now.

So it is that in this place my thoughts dwell upon beauty and upon the responsibilities of leadership. The Way of Beauty and the Way of Power are essential considerations for our return to Creation.

There is an expression in our language: *wuniish.* It is not possible to translate exactly. It would take many English words to convey the feeling of that word. Its base is *wunny,* which means beautiful. *Wunny* is also used as an exclamation of delight and approval. As an expression of parting, people say in English "goodbye," "stay well" or "have a good one". We say *"Wuniish,"* It is much more powerful. It has the connotation of "Stay beautiful" or "Walk in beauty" or "May Beauty surround you."

What is Beauty? Human beings are the only ones on this planet who ask that question and are moved by beauty. The ancient wisdom of our people instructs us that the perception of beauty is a special gift. It was given to human beings to show them the Sacred Path.

Our comprehension of beauty grows as we grow. I can now see the beauty in many things that I thought ugly when I was young. Things I once thought of as beautiful I now perceive as ugly – that is, shallow, false, or deadening. What is Beauty? Beauty is the great harmony in the Song of Creation.

The words Love and Beauty identify feelings of a similar spiritual source. What they describe is a recognition of rightness, of harmony. When you love someone, it is the recognition of how right and perfect his or her being is in a universe that is right and perfect. When you see something as beautiful you are recognizing the harmony with which it fits into all of Creation. Of course, that is only possible in contradiction to a sense of wrongness and disharmony. Our plant and animal relatives act only out of their Original Instructions and so have no sense of right or wrong, harmony or disharmony. But human beings, given minds capable of making choices, can choose to do things which produce destructive, inharmonious, unloving and unbeautiful results. So it is that we have been given these feelings of Love and Beauty to guide these minds of ours that are otherwise simply computers with no built-in value program other than that of their own survival.

If you put enough information into these mind computers to show that the survival of the individual depends upon the cooperative efforts of human beings to create a harmonious society, along with the information about how we create conflict within and among ourselves, then our minds will arrive at the logically correct conclusions about how to achieve that harmony. But in this very complex world, that takes a lot more education than most people get.

The ones who are the clearest about the folly of computer–mind thinking are the little children. I go to schools and camps and other gatherings not only to tell stories to the children, but also to listen to them. They ask, why don't people stop fighting? Why don't they sit together and work with each other? Why aren't they kind to each other? The letters they write to the leaders of the countries are wiser than all of those leaders' deliberations. Their minds have not yet been conditioned. They feel the Original Instructions still.

That is what I mean by walking in a sacred manner. It is acting in a way that enhances Creation. To walk in beauty is to follow the universal principles of harmony and cooperation. It is to live every moment in love.

As Metacomet sat here on his stone seat gazing out on the beauty of the world before him, I wonder what thoughts came into his mind. His father, the Massasoit Ousemequin, had been born into a society that had endeavored to maintain beauty and harmony for thousands of years. But in the lifetime of Metacomet a new and disruptive element had appeared in this world. A strange people from another land far away had come and had been greeted by his father with traditional hospitality and generosity. This was according to the Original Instructions which his people understood. But the strangers did not understand the same Instructions. They acted, not as neighbors, but as superiors, as conquerors, governors and judges. They preached their religion and converted whole villages to their ways. By the time Metacomet became the massasoit, or supreme sachem, the greed, intolerance, and injustice of the invaders had become intolerable. His own brother had died in captivity as the Pilgrims attempted to impress their authority upon him.

Metacomet was the leader of his nation, of the Wampanoag Federation, and he had much to consider. This was a situation which had never occurred in the history of this people and this land. He had no precedent by which to guide his thoughts. Conquest and ownership of land by individuals was unknown. It took fifty–five years for his people to under-stand the real intentions of the invaders. By then, many of his tribes were converted to "praying (Christianized) Indians" and allied to the English, and much of the traditional land under the care of his people had been appropriated, bought or seized. What should he do?

At this point I want to discuss what power and leader-ship mean in the ways of our people. There is a fundamental difference in the concept of power held by people who live the way of the circle and those who live the way of the pyramid.

The weight of the pyramid presses downwards from the top to the bottom. What holds it in place is fear and the force of its structure. On the top is the emperor, the king, the president — the boss (I use the male form deliber-ately . . . because even when these happen to be females, they are part of an essentially male–dominated system). Under him are the palace guards, the police, the army, the goon squads that keep the leader in place. Then come priests, nobles, merchants, professionals, who are allowed a superior position over workers, peasants, servants, and slaves, upon whom the whole weight of the system rests. This is the way of domination. It is created and maintained by fear. The oppressed fear the power of the oppressors; the oppressors fear the potential power of the oppressed. This is why there is such irrational fear of communism in capitalist countries and such irrational fear of capitalism in communist countries.

What holds a circle in place is not a pressure from outside, but an attraction from inside, an attraction towards the center. This centripetal force, call it love, call it spiritual coherence, call it what you will, is very real. It is not a matter for conjecture and dispute. In the circle each en-hances the circle and is enhanced by it. So the power of the circle is the power of harmony with the way of Creation.

People who live in the way of the circle understand power, not as domination, not as power *over*, but as power *with;* not power in conflict, but rather in harmony with Creation. They understand that the idea of power over na-ture or over people is power in contradiction to itself, since everything is part of the whole. Such power is destructive and, ultimately, self–destructive. Such power is therefore an illusion. That is what we mean when we say that the only real power is spiritual power. Power does not reside in guns and gold. That is the error which all the governmental and economic leaders of the world continue to make. That's why the history of the political and economic dynasties of civilization are stories of rise and fall, of continuous failure. The only true power is that which functions within the Original Instructions, that is in harmony with and enhances Creation. That is the power of love and the Way of Beauty.

How does this understanding of power affect our concept of leadership? Naturally a leader in the way of the circle does not exert or expect power over the circle. Such a leader is rather an instrument of love and of the people's desires for harmony and health.

Leadership is thought of as responsibility. It is a response to the needs of the circle. Since all are equal in the circle, it is the responsibility of each one to think as a leader and to support leadership that enhances the health and harmony of the circle. Of course that circle is not only the village or nation, but extends to all of Creation, since all is one circle. A leader, then, is simply one who can tune in to the circle of the people, as well as all of Creation, and take the initiative to protect the harmony and enhance the creativity of that circle.

If we think of people as naturally competitive, we will create and reinforce that attitude and fill our social interactions with struggle and alienation. If we understand that harmony is the larger law of Creation and that human beings are naturally cooperative, we will inspire that attitude in others and our interactions will be filled with closeness and mutual support.

There is a general misconception about how leadership worked for the first people of this land. When Europeans dealt with native leaders, European concepts were applied to those roles. Thus they called our supreme sachems "kings" (with some irony, since they thought they were ignorant and savage and expected to dominate them). Wamsutta they named for Alexander the Great, and Metacomet was called after Alexander's father, King Philip of Macedon.

But our chiefs were not kings, or tyrants, not even benevolent autocrats. Their functions were to comprehend the will of the people and coordinate their activities. The quality of their leadership was shown in how well they could communicate and clarify issues, and especially how well they could inspire others by their integrity, justness, courage, and love for their people.

At West Point Military Academy they have taught the military tactics of the Nez Percé, Chief Joseph. What they perhaps do not know is that Joseph was in opposition to the basic course his people took. But like all great leaders he listened to all the people, the chiefs, the elders, the warriors, the women. Joseph spoke out for what he believed, for what he thought was right. Although his heart was in his home valley of the Wallowa, he was forced by circumstances beyond his control to fight and run. Like a true leader he thought first of his people and always contrived to do his utmost for them. If it had not been for the telegraph and the ubiquity of the U.S. Army arrayed against him, he would have brought his people safely to Canada to try to make a new life, safe from U.S. oppression.

The great chief Crazy Horse was described by his young cousin Black Elk as thinking only of his people, not of himself at all, to the extent that if there were not enough food he would fast so that there would be more for others. He never made rash decisions, but listened to others and pondered and contemplated long the course he should follow for the greatest good of his people.

So, I have heard, it was with all the great native leaders among the many nations. Sometimes in the old legends there are stories of cruel and dictatorial chiefs, but not in the times that people can remember, so I think those stories were told as teachings and cautions to the young about how to live and to lead in a good way.

Our sachems had councils of elders, or *paneises*, who in turn listened to the clan mothers who consolidated the wisdom of the women. Before a sachem proposed any action, the thoughts and feelings of all were heard and a consensus arrived at in council.

If, in rare circumstances, a chief might be so arbitrary, so incorrect or so unheeding of the ideas and needs of his people that they would give up trying to correct him, they would not need a revolution to get rid of him. Some peoples had procedures, such as in the Great Law of Peace of the Houdenosonie, wherewith the clan mothers, representing the women, would remove the chief's horns of office. In most other places, the offending chief would simply wake up one morning to find that all his band had gone away and left him alone.

So it was that when the people became divided by the new ways of the Europeans, they had not the unity to deal effectively with this threat to their way of life. The great Passaconaway of this land now called New Hampshire saw that, and it broke his heart. In different times and places great leaders tried to fight back to save their people — Metacomet, Powhattan, Pontiac, Tecumseh, Oceola, Black Hawk, Geronimo, Captain Jack — without the unity of all their people or knowledge of the true nature of the threat. When treaties were made by the United States they were often made with individual chiefs who had no power to make such treaties for their people. In the long run that didn't matter, since the European–American governments have not kept any of the treaties they made with native nations anyway.

Later the foreign governments created a governmental system like their own among the native nations. These so-called tribal councils and band councils are patterned on adversary, competitive political models of the Europeans, unlike the old councils that sought the unity and consensus of all. You must understand how destructive it is to bring this competitive system of conflict and alienation among a people that have known only harmony and cooperation, and who have been stripped of their lands and resources and their right of self–determination. Council membership becomes sought for the money and power, instead of being a responsibility of dedicated spiritual service to the people and Creation.

I remember how I felt at one time before I learned of this very ancient wisdom of my people. I saw the destructiveness of the powers of the world and the follies of its leaders, and I thought that leadership in itself was inherently bad. I saw, as Lord Acton had said, that power corrupts, and I wanted no part of it. I understood power as he did, as the dominant culture did. I thought, "Let there be no more leaders. Let us join hands and go forward side by side."

But I had no experience of living in a true circle of equals at that time. When I began to do that there were more than forty winters behind me. In our first circles we tried to live without leadership. Doing that made me reconsider my ideas. Leadership, as I said before, is just responsibility. When there is no leadership in a circle, no one is taking responsibility. Things are neglected or left unfinished or badly thought out. People start saying, "That's not my job," or "Why doesn't anybody ever clean the kitchen?" Or take out the garbage. Or mend the broken door. Or cut firewood in spring.

Eventually there's someone who can't stand it any more, who shows initiative and responsibility and gets things done. Now everyone can say, "Oh, that's her job," and not have to think about it any more. Those who assume responsibility get more and more of it dumped on them, until they are burnt out and quit. So leadership still doesn't look very

desirable, only a necessary evil.

In a small circle it becomes very clear that everyone needs to think of herself as responsible. Everyone needs to be a leader. Otherwise it becomes exhaustively oppressive for the one or the few who do take responsibility. They get abandoned, feel overloaded and isolated. They get resented, even attacked. They are doing something good for everyone, and no one makes it easier for them. They are rarely appreciated. What they need is the support of the circle, people thinking well of them and helping with the common tasks. They need everyone to assume responsibility and to think as a leader. For efficiency, leadership may specialize and focus on limited areas. But it really helps if everyone in the circle makes a conscious decision to support the circle by thinking of its needs and to support those who commit themselves to the coordination of the circle's activities in any given area. In a circle where all have shared and clarified their common spiritual vision, this is not difficult. In a system of competition and power over others, it is virtually impossible.

Having rediscovered this truth about the true nature of leadership, we have begun to learn a few other things that enhance leadership in the way of the circle.

In a circle, everyone is a leader. That means every person takes personal responsibility for the whole circle. Taking responsibility means thinking about what is needed and communicating that thinking to the circle. It does not mean doing all the work yourself. Being a leader, taking responsibility, means seeing that what needs to get done gets done. It means doing whatever it takes to get the job done. That could be doing it all yourself, or it could be delegating it to others, eliciting support, encouraging, cajoling, inspiring, demonstrating.

In both a circle and a pyramid there needs to be one person coordinating every activity. The difference is that in a true circle the coordinator expects everyone to take responsibility for the whole group, to think about the group and what needs to be done, and to communicate those thoughts to the coordinator. The coordinator has the benefit of her colleagues' thinking and can choose the best actions for the group. If the members' ideas are in conflict, the leader may wish to facilitate a council which will brainstorm and find the most elegant solution. There may be times when the leader will just have to rely on her own best judgment and decide on a certain course for the group. The weight of that decision need not be onerous. Sometimes the only way to learn is to go ahead and make a mistake. That's fine too.

Now I want to talk directly to you. Yes, you personally. What are you doing with your life? I assume that however good it is, you would like to make it better. I know there are places where the world rubs hard on you and makes your life have less of the ease and joy it could. I know your life could stand to have more love in it, more fun in it, more creative success in it, and more beauty in it. All of us would prefer to live without the threat of nuclear war, without the threat of crime and violence all around us, without the loneliness and alienation that haunts our days and nights.

What would you think if I said that developing your leadership is the way to all of those things? I would like you to consider now the possibility of your taking leadership and making things the way you want them to be. If that seems overwhelming or impossible, just stay with me a little longer.

I have watched and listened and learned from my elders before me, and I have gone forth to make my own mistakes and learn from them too. I have helped to put together gatherings and movements of thousands of people, taught leadership to hundreds of others, and co–created a cooperative community that functions lovingly and well. In all of these I have learned a few very important things that will be of use to you.

A world of beauty, a society of love, a life of abundance and joy are not mere fantasies. They are totally possible, assured, in fact, if the human race lasts long enough for everyone to learn the information we are sharing together here. Such a paradise is what Creation was meant to be, and all it requires is for us to apply what we already know. But we have to get going and move humanity quickly in that direction, because the threat of extinction on this planet is very real and very imminent. The Purification prophesied by many of our old ones is inevitable. The only question is whether it means that we change or that we are obliterated.

Most people are aware of this crisis on some level. A few people are teaching and organizing to avert at least some part of it. Some have just decided to get what they can for themselves and let what happens happen. "Eat, drink, and be merry." I suspect that most people are terrified deep inside, but have shut off that terror because it seems hopeless and too painful. They are paralyzed and cannot even think of solutions. They feel it's all too big and complicated for one person to have any effect. The forces of destruction are too powerful and too entrenched. Those allied with these forces do not see them as destructive. In fact, they are so terrified that they believe only their rigidity and the threat of violence can save us from destruction.

Because of this there is a great void in effective human leadership, and this world of ours drifts on an unheeded course towards extinction. Look around your world. In your community, in your town, in your state or nation, on the international scene, where do you see the leaders who, in the hearts of their constituents, inspire change — change in the directions of peace, justice, love, cooperation, beauty and all the things we know are right?

I am going to suggest that your leadership abilities have not yet been uncovered. They are still under wraps, hidden even from you. If your full natural leadership were being exercised, if your true potential were in full force, I would know about you. You would be a shining light and a beacon to the world. Similarly, if I had developed all the potential that is my birthright as a human being I would have changed the world long ere now. I am working on it — seeing to my own circles quite well now, and expanding them all the time. Perhaps if we work together on this we can help each other.

The fact is that everyone is a potential leader, and a good one. It is part of being human, part of our Original Instructions to be caretakers of the earth. Not to be dominators, but caretakers, custodians. But almost nobody is living up to her potential as an effective human leader. Why is that?

Well, what gets in *your* way?

Perhaps, like myself, you developed a resistance to the whole idea of leadership on account of bad experiences with leaders and authorities. We have been quite correct in being suspicious and questioning authority, given the history of civilization and where it has led so far. It is really hard for me to explain my concept of leadership in Germany, for example. In their language the word for leader is *fuehrer*, the title adopted by Adolf Hitler. That's enough to make anyone shy of leadership.

But that was not human leadership. That was distressed leadership. Remember, there are two basic human emotions, love and fear. Hitler acted completely out of fear, and as a result created devotion in those who had the same fears and evoked terror and rage in all the rest of the world. If he had had the opportunity to express and heal his own terror and rage at an early age, he could have been an effective, loving, human leader.

This resistance to leadership made me seek out groups that expressed opposition to leaders. For a while I thought we were doing great without leaders. But then I began to notice that whenever we did something well, there was always a leader — not in title, but someone who quietly took responsibility and did the thinking that was necessary to get the job done, presented proposals, asked for help, inspired and encouraged others. I noticed that different people were drawn to coordinate different projects, and that they trained others to do their functions and rotated into other jobs. Whether or not anyone carries the designation of leader, every project needs to have one person thinking about what is needed and coordinating, inspiring, and organizing. It's good if everyone in the group is thinking as a leader, but it is essential that at least one person do that. It is a good idea for any leader to encourage the leadership of everyone in her group. The more people thinking and inspiring others, the better.

So I would like you to put aside all resistance you may have had and admit that deep inside you are a leader. The world needs you. I need you. We need your support in changing the world, and we also need you to train other leaders. We have a lot of work to do, and we need to get moving.

It's your world. You are the center of your universe. Creation put you there to take charge of it. It's in your nature to be a leader. It's time for you to take responsibility. For how much? For all of it! What? The whole universe? Right. It's your universe. You are responsible for it all. Your responsibility has no limits.

"Wait a minute," you say, "I can't handle all that. Any way," you may think, "it's not in my hands. . . . Only God can be in charge of it all." Listen. Creation developed *your* mind, *your* heart and *your* will to take charge. No, you don't own the place, but you are the custodian.

The job is not as vast as it might seem. First you take care of yourself. Get yourself warm and fed and rested enough to have all your energy intact. Then you naturally look around for something more to do. You take care of your environment and the people you live with, your family first, then your community. If you never leave home, your influence will spread from there across the universe. If you dedicate your life to keeping one place beautiful and helping a handful of people to realize their full potentials, you will be as powerful and as effective as any leader who influences millions of people directly. But if you choose to go beyond that, by winning allies and supporters, there are no limits to what you can create in the world.

So now what gets in your way? A lot of people say, "I'm just not cut out to be a leader." That's buying the notion that some people are born leaders and some aren't. The fact is, we were all born leaders, only something happened to us, and we lost it. What happened is that we got hurt as children when we received messages that we were inadequate in one way or another. Then we saw a lot of people becoming leaders for the wrong reasons: to get love, attention, to escape, to get admiration and appreciation. Some of us were told our thinking and ideas were stupid and wrong. Some of us were told we were lazy or selfish or greedy. Even when those voices were gone we carried them with us, believing them, believing we were inadequate, not smart enough, not good enough. We are afraid of responsibility because we might make a mistake and get blamed and humiliated the way we did when we were young.

If you have such ideas about yourself still, you need to understand they are all wrong, and they are holding you back. It's not easy to throw off a life-time habit of self-doubt in an instant, but if you understand how wrong those self-doubting thoughts are, you are on the way. You can commit yourself to stepping boldly forth as a leader. All your old terror will come up, but step forth anyway, shaking and laughing and telling everyone you are scared to death but you are taking charge. You will find many to support you, and your scorned fear will begin to loosen its hold on you.

You already have all the resources you need to be a good human leader. Your first resource is your understanding that Creation is good and is working through you to be better and better. That's evolution. The people who share this world are also basically good and are potential allies for you when you break through their barriers of distress and isolation. Your intelligence is a major resource available to you. You can always think. And your ability to make a decision will keep you from ever being stuck.

In my workshops, training people to take charge of their lives and the world, to become healers and teachers and leaders, I have a game I introduce as a tribal dance. Do you remember the children's game "Follow the leader"? That is what we do as a dance with a hat. I tell everyone they must dance in imitation of whoever is wearing the hat. When each person gets the hat she moves and plays and watches everyone else being her until she has explored her own creativity in movement enough and passes the hat on to someone else who hasn't yet had it. I always love to watch this dance. I see people who have the idea they can't dance become outstandingly creative under the attention of others. I see people who are shy, who never talk, who retreat from any leadership, suddenly become new people under the hat and the respectful observation of their peers. They leap boldly out and delight in having everyone do graceful, expressive, funny, and wildly impossible movements. It's a wonderful game, showing that leadership can be fun. I offer it for your next gathering of friends. Watch the natural leadership in people surge to the fore.

Please realize that you are a powerful person. Where does your power reside? It resides in the fact that at every moment in your life there are a multitude of options, and you are completely free to choose any of them. Whenever you feel stuck, when things seem hopeless, remember you are free right then to choose a new point of view, one that serves you better, that makes you more powerful, more loving, more relaxed, more enthusiastic, more creative, or whatever you want to be.

Maybe you don't want to be a leader because you have held leadership responsibility before, and it wasn't any fun. You worried about everything, had to fight to maintain your authority, got cut down or blamed by others, or you had to do everything yourself if you wanted it done right. It's exhausting. I can understand. Leadership that way is hard.

But we don't have to set it up that way. You don't have to be a martyr or a tyrant or a workaholic to be a leader. Good leaders know how to pace themselves, to vary their work and to enjoy what they do, to play heartily, to rest deeply, and to get the help and support they need. Good human leadership is refreshing.

Thinking about a group beyond yourself is refreshing. It empowers your creativity. If you inspire others with your confidence and enthusiasm, you can delegate the work to others. People don't like to be ordered around, but they do appreciate being asked for help. People are naturally cooperative. When they are not under stress, they are natural allies for you and for each other.

What does an effective human leader do?

F irst, a leader inspires. She shows confidence and inspires confidence in others. She can communicate the value of the work to be done and the ability of the people to do it. She has integrity. Her words and her actions are consistent with each other. Her information is correct. She is committed to the group and to the task at hand. She is decisive and courageous and has stamina, but is also flexible and open–minded. She encourages the leadership of the others in the group. Above all, a leader loves not only the group, but each person it in, and she shows it. She breaks through the isolation which accompanies all our distress. She holds the highest expectation for each member, knowing how capable and brilliant they are. She appreciates them in public, and she helps each one with getting rid of whatever is getting in her way. She inspires love with her love.

I know that's not what a lot of people who are supposedly experts in business and government think that leadership is, but when I see really effective human leadership in operation, and it's fairly rare, *that's* what it is. Those experts still have a lot to learn. The new teachers of management skills are now stressing the values of cooperation, of paying attention to and eliciting the best thinking from all the workers. This has led to increased efficiency and output. I haven't heard of any teacher daring enough yet, however, to suggest that managers should actually love their workers!

What are the tools you need to be an effective human leader? Maybe the most important is listening. You can't think *for* a group of people, so you need to hear their thinking. You may be the one to organize and coordinate their activities, but most often they will have a good idea of what is needed in their department of the task. A variety of insights always gives you a broader picture, but there is another important reason why learning to listen, listen, listen is all–important. Everyone is walking around with a lot of unexpressed feelings that they are eager to share with anyone who will pay attention to them for a few minutes. Even men who find it impossible to show their feelings can easily be encouraged to talk about something in which they are very interested and into which they have feelings invested. People have a natural intuition that expressing these feelings is healing for them, but, outside of therapists and clerics, there are few people willing to listen. Everyone is trying to tell you their problems. Successful hairdressers, bartenders, and cabdrivers have learned the value of listening, and people really let out all their problems on them.

There are two important reasons for you to listen to the

feelings of people in your group. The first is that unexpressed feelings dominate people's consciousness and keep
them from their best thinking. The second is that it is an
act of love and caring, and you will be highly regarded and
sought after as a friend and counselor, which makes your
work as leader that much easier.

Another important leadership tool is the art of communication. A leader can articulate her concepts and ideas
clearly, express goals in a way that excites and inspires, and
encourage confidence, cooperation and affection in the group
and for each individual.

Perhaps the most important tool is yourself. Your own
confidence, your own willingness to tackle the job, your
enthusiasm for the work, your affection and respect for your
co-workers, your courage and good humor, these all help set
the tone of the group and the work. You also need an
awareness of the past history of the group, a good grasp of
the present situation, what is required now, and an inspiring
vision of the future — an exciting and worthwhile goal.

Good human leadership means encouraging and bringing
out the leadership potential in others, having the highest expectations for all that they can be. It means thinking well,
not only of the group, but of each individual in the group,
finding what's getting in their way, and helping them grow
into their full potential as leaders. A good leader will welcome a bright, new, potential leader. If someone looks like
she is out for your job, you will rejoice! That's just what you
have been looking for. You want to train someone as soon as
possible to take over for you, so you can move on and create
new, more challenging and interesting work for yourself in
the world, and teach her to do the same.

A good leader will take responsibility to change any
feelings of powerlessness she may have, realizing it is completely in her power to choose her point of view, including
that of being capable of handling any task worth doing. She
will not blame any external conditions for her impotence. She
will not wait for someone else to do it, someone who "knows
better" or "whose job it is" or "who has more power." She
will eliminate any dependency she may have on others,
which stems from feelings of powerlessness. This includes
dependencies on lovers, systems, government, and God
Herself. However, a good leader will make allies for herself
and for her group among other groups and other leaders.
She will take responsible leadership in every area of her life
— at home, at work, in relationships, in community, nations
and in the world. And she will decide to enjoy it all, to live

every moment well and have fun.

As a teacher and a leader you yourself will begin to learn and to grow at a faster rate. Thinking of a group, of other people, of expanded possibilities makes your life richer and more interesting. Your understanding and creativity grow apace. In these days of crisis for our world, I am less interested in simply healing individuals so they can function well, and more interested in training people to be teachers and leaders who will teach others to be teachers and leaders and quickly bring an end to all violence, hunger, poverty, oppression, and injustice in the world.

Does that sound like a task worthy of you?

I f it does, I am with you. I commit myself to be your ally and supporter in leading your universe to be the human paradise we all want it to be. Remembering that real power is not power over but power drawn from harmony with the Creation, let us walk together in a sacred manner upon a path of Beauty.

I can't guarantee that you won't make mistakes, and that it will all be easy. I *can* guarantee it will be the most interesting and challenging game you could find to play for the precious time of your life. Walking a Path of Beauty, the beauty and the power of your human essence will radiate from you, and others will want to know what it is you know and what you do to make you the way you are. If you have a circle, they will want to participate, and they will learn and grow from that, and perhaps want to start their own circles, which will create other circles in turn.

I am completely confident that together we will change the world. Together there is nothing we cannot do.

Chapter Eight

I Awake!
I Live!

The sun has long descended beyond the western rim of the world, draining the last rosy color from the horizon and from the wave-tops of the darkling bay. Evening is settling into night, and the sunset wind has quieted to a soft breeze.

We are standing on the curling wave-crest of a sand dune. Above our heads glitters a brilliant panoply of stars. They are tiny sparks glowing on the dark floor of night. How large? How far?

There is no moon yet, no clouds. From the unseen shore beyond, the steady muffled surge of the ocean crumbles and smears itself along the shore in the beckoning dark. Everywhere I travel on this round world, I can always feel at home if I can find my way to the shore and stand on rocks or sand to hear and smell and watch the pulsing presence of the sea. To grow up on the dunes as I did is never to forget the changeable evanescence of the land and the atavistic pull of the ancient and eternal ocean. We live on the earth, on shifting rock and sand, but the sea is in our blood.

So many grains of sand, so many drops of water, so many different species of living creatures, so many individuals of our species on one tiny world that is but a grain of sand, a scattered spark, a drop of water in the vast ocean of the universe.

Questions fill our minds. What is all this for? What is it

doing? There are billions of galaxies, each with billions of stars like those we see around us in the night sky, and all are spinning through the unthinkable distances of space. The light from some of these stars, billions of years old, has taken hundreds of years, thousands of years to reach us. The smudge of light from that little blur up there above the Great Medicine Wheel has taken two million years to get here from a neighboring galaxy. We stare up and back into time.

Faced with such immensity of time and space, what is the significance of our brief lifespan on this mote of star–ash?

What is a human being?

A human being is one who can ask such questions on such a night, and who must ask them, even though no answer could carry any certainty at this stage of our development. Each person must ask for herself or himself alone. If the reply that issues from the silence of the blazing firmament or from the dark rhythm of the tides resonates through our being, we may trust that as a mysterious truth and a guide.

I am in touch with Creation everywhere, on a mountaintop, in a forest glade, in a meadow or a desert. But nowhere so vividly and intensely as by the sea, or on it. The most powerful and profound time for this connection is on a clear night when there is no moon, only an infinity of stars above the dark and sounding sea. I am reminded of our Creation story, of a mysterious time before there was an earth or a sky, a sun or a moon, only a world full of light, the light of billions of fires, and the spirits of those fires, and below them the black and lightless waters, moving and murmuring with the spirits of the dark. On such a night it is easy to feel we are present at a very early scene in the story of Creation. The scene seems to wait for a questioning mind to enter and fulfill it.

What is the purpose of human existence?

Among all the varieties of beings, our own species is the only one that asks such a question. And because we can ask it, it seems we must ask it. Creation has given to human beings an inborn curiosity. We not only need to feed and reproduce, we need to know, to explore, to investigate, discover, probe, pry, experiment, and learn, learn, learn. Why is that? It must be part of our purpose.

The purpose of human existence, it seems, is to live, to grow, to survive, and to ask the purpose of human existence. To ask. To seek knowledge.

The scientist is not the only seeker of knowledge. The farmer, the worker, the merchant, the artist, the healer, the lover, the parent, and, above all, the child also seek it. Curiosity, the search for truth, is an essential part of all human activity.

Human beings are creatures of body, mind, heart and spirit. We have certain physical, mental, emotional, and spiritual capacities. We are capable of extending these capacities beyond anything that we have ever dreamed. I believe we are capable of infinite expansion. And that, a chorus of celestial fires in an expanding universe around us affirms, is the purpose of our existence.

Creation is a condition of continuous change. Through this cosmic expanse stars are born, have their lives, and die. Here on earth, whole species are born, have their lives, and become extinct. Or else they are transformed into a stronger, smarter kind. The human species has had several such past lives. They are reflected in many of our ancient tales of former worlds.

Now the human species has gotten itself trapped in the web of institutions known as modern civilization. Unless we transform ourselves once more and our whole destructive culture as well, we may soon be as extinct as the dinosaur or the passenger pigeon.

The business of living creatures is, as the old saying goes, to live and learn, to become more conscious, more aware. Most human beings are asleep most of their lives. What marvels, what a life we could manifest if all of us were functioning at our highest peak of attentive awareness all of the time! Instead, we are in a daze, hypnotized by our culture, our conditioning, our parenting, our schooling, mesmerized by the baubles of our civilization, numbed and made stupid by all our institutions. We perform our work in a trance. We eat, communicate minimally with each other, listen to music, read the newspaper, watch television, drive the car, travel far over the earth. Still we are only half "there." We are not present. We are on automatic, like robots.

When we fall in love we wake up for a while — to that relationship, if to nothing else. When we are with our beloved, colors are brighter, food is tastier, sounds are clearer, everything is more vivid and memorable. We are totally attentive to our beloved. After a while the power of that magic generally wears off in the stupefying realities of everyday living, and most people return to their normal half–conscious state.

The great holy people, saints and mystics, are those who stay in love with everyone, with all Creation, all the time. They are totally tuned in to all the relationships in the universe every instant of their lives. They are awake. They are truly alive.

What is it that keeps us from being totally in love with all of Creation all of the time? Since that is the condition to which we seem to aspire, a condition of total bliss and total awareness, and since we see that some people have achieved that, it must be the proper and natural condition for our species. Total bliss and total awareness are our natural and proper condition! What a powerful suggestion that is! What is it that keeps us from being that?

In a word, it is fear. That is what the old ones learned and taught.

I t begins when we are conceived, as we absorb the fears that our mothers experience during pregnancy. It is advanced further by the travail and shock of birth. It is reinforced by frightening experiences in a new strange world, by our parents, our schools, our friends and our lovers as we grow. If we were not isolated during these early times of terror, if there was someone there to hold us and to hear us scream, to let us shake and cry and laugh through our fears, then we would emerge from that terror clear and strong and sure of ourselves.

That was the function of the circle in traditional tribal society, of the extended family, the clan, and the village. There was always someone there to heal and guide the young person, to help and encourage, through ceremony and ritual, to learn to understand and to cope with fear and confusion. But too often in these times there is no one there and the fear is driven deep into us as we struggle somehow to survive through all that assaults us. Each recurrence of threat recalls the old terrors, and we learn to shut down our feelings, our thinking and our awareness. We feel vulnerable. Anything can get to us. Hierarchies, authorities, the government, the boss, the head office, the police, the rebels, strangers, whites, blacks, weirdos, foreigners, others.

Crime, poverty, violence, world tension, hatred, fear and suspicion are all around us. We are hurt. We are terrified.

We are withdrawn. Throw on the automatic pilot and hang up a sign, "out to lunch." We don't want to know. We don't want to talk about it. Keep it light. If it gets too insistent we can always buy relief. There is alcohol, Seconol, Valium, marijuana, cocaine, television, bingo, tourism, food, and sex. Yes, we even make love fearfully, guardedly, numbly. Sex becomes another place to hide for a time.

To expose ourselves and feel all our feelings is terrifying. Yet, if we ever do anything with all our full conscious attention it makes the rest of our lives seem pale and dull, and we remember that moment always.

We are not only part of Creation, we are Creation, striving for ever greater consciousness. We must bring this evolving consciousness to our every deed, beginning with the beginning. To sexuality and conception, to gestation and birthing.

The use of female contraceptives has allowed men to become even more unconscious in the sexual act. One of the positive effects of the great horror of the AIDS epidemic may be to make men — and women — more conscious and decisive in their sexual activity. That may be part of the balance that Creation needs, and it is forcing us to get smart and take responsibility or perish. Notice, it says to us, the power and the depth and the consequence of the sexual act.

Sexuality throbs through all of life. From the moment of our birth we are profoundly sexual beings. Sexual energy is omnipresent in everything around us at all times. Our relationship to the environment is deeply erotic. Sexuality gives us the potential for a more acute awareness of splendor and ecstasy in every moment. But because this energy is so powerful it can have a devastating effect when it is distorted and abused. And because contemporary society is so out of balance, so full of fear, conflict, violence and oppression, as well as greed, attachment to the material and superficial, and just sheer loneliness and despair, our sexuality is everywhere distorted and abused. It is inevitable that, growing up in this fearsome and irrational society, our earliest sexual feelings, thoughts, and experiences are beset with anxiety, hurt, misunderstanding and misinformation.

The whole culture is sexually warped. Sexuality is manipulated to sell products, and sold for its own sake in the media. Artificial standards of beauty and sexual attraction are promulgated everywhere. A traveler from space would conclude that this world is sex–crazed, with all our clothing, furnishing, automobile design, food, drink, entertainment and social interaction dictated by our insatiable hunger for sexual fulfillment.

It is noteworthy that young people brought up in our traditional native cultures, while being more self–sufficient and self–reliant at an earlier age, do not display sexual desire until a much later time — a time more appropriate to the bearing and raising of children, and that this desire is felt in a more rational context.

No doubt we shall not heal the sexual sickness of society until we purge it of domination, competition, greed, and alienation; until we reshape it towards equality, cooperation, and love. Meanwhile, to heal ourselves individually we must become conscious of the ways we have been hurt, express those feelings, and let them go. With greater consciousness comes greater freedom and naturalness, ease and comfort in our bodies and emotions, and sensitive alertness in our thinking.

At the lowest level of consciousness, sex is just a powerful energy, blind and insistent. At the next level there is a consciousness of delight, of joy and abandon — sheer play. At the next level there is a consciousness of the partner's feelings and desires. The play enriches the wonder of communication, separate beings exploring themselves exploring each other. Then there comes a consciousness of love. Finally there is a consciousness of the effect of this act upon one's family and friends, upon the human beings that may be created, upon the environment, the animal and plant life, upon the human race and the planet, upon the cosmos and all of Creation.

O ur lives really have no beginning and no end, only times to stop and mark the changes and celebrate. The beings we are were fashioned at the Dawn of Creation. Perhaps there were dawns before that one. Perhaps there are many universes evolving eternally. We cannot know. But one thing is certain — our lives did not begin in our mothers' wombs. We are star–stuff, which we received from our ancestors, and which we pass on to the generations to come, for we are now the ancestors of the yet unborn.

The conception of life is one of the important marking points of life which we need to approach with the consciousness of prayer. Whenever we come together as a man and woman to join in sexual union, it would be well for us to begin with a prayer of communion, between ourselves, and with Creation. If a seed is to be planted it is best done with great love and clarity. The future of the life that grows must be carefully considered. It is important that the relationship between the woman and the man be clear and loving at this time, that the environment and relationships of the mother be supportive during the nine months before birth. Human society begins with the determination of the man to provide this protection and care for the woman at this time. The beginning of family is the beginning of community. The child growing in the womb is a child of the community, and all should assist in maintaining that supportive environment.

The men of the community recognize that the business of carrying, birthing, and nursing a child is the responsibility of the woman. The men take their cues from the women on how best to provide a safe and nurturing environment for this mother and her child. One of the crazy imbalances of civilization is the fact that male doctors claim to know more than women about the processes of gestation, birth, and nursing, which men can only know externally, by observation and studying texts. Women carry this knowledge in their genes, the inherited experience of a million generations of human birth. In our traditional communities this knowledge is part of the tribal experience, taught and consecrated by ritual and ceremony.

Our humanity and our connection with life begins in the womb and is profoundly influenced by the passage we call birth. For us to bring that humanity and natural connection back to our communities, the women must once again take control of the processes of pregnancy and birth, and the men must support the women in this.

While our babies are in the womb, the mothers must be able to perceive their environment as safe, loving and joyful, so that a feeling of trust and happiness is transmitted to the baby. The birth may be prepared for with the same objective, to provide the most accepting, gentle, caring entry into the new world of light and air and sound. The transition can be as conscious and sacred as a prayer, gentle and quiet and loving. The mother and experienced midwives are the ones who understand best how to achieve this, and the father and other men will follow their wishes.

The use of drugs in obstetrics deprives women of the most profoundly conscious and intensely vital moments of their lives and no doubt has an effect upon the child as well. Sometimes such use cannot be helped, but we need to understand that time must be taken then to recover the feelings that have been buried by that process, to get mother and child fully present again.

The womb is like a dream world, dark and warm, the reassuring rhythm of the mother's heart providing the beat
for the dance of life while other sounds are muffled and
distant. Coming into the world is an abrupt awakening.
Quickly the infant must cope with new images of light, new
sounds, the burning sensation of air and the skill of breathing. Suddenly the little fish must be transformed into a little
animal.

The little fish has grown trusting in the safety of the
womb. The little animal awakes to a new world, trusting the
safety of that environment as it had come to trust the other.
This is the natural process. Thousands and thousands of
generations of birthing provide that expectation in the baby.
How the trust and love of that baby will grow now depends
very much on this transition. The baby expects to be en-
folded at the mother's breast, hearing the familiar beat of her
heart in order to know all is well.

The first ceremony of your life is the moment you were
conceived. The second is the moment of your birth. The way
the parents relate to those moments is of great importance
to how this baby will grow and relate to herself, to the
community, to the earth, and to the Creation. The strength
and quality of the community's life are greatly affected by the
way that those ceremonies are regarded and marked.

For me as a man, seeking to understand what it means
to be a man, to be a male human consciousness, I find
the answer in my response to women, and in the demand of
future generations for my support and nurture during pregnancy, birth and the raising of children. As a human being
striving for consciousness, what I mean by the concept of
spirituality, by the mystic connection of myself to the Creation, is most powerfully illuminated in the moment of birth.

I can best transmit this feeling to you, perhaps, by
looking within myself, to my own experience. I would like to
tell you the story of the birth of my first child.

When I met the mother of my children fifteen years ago, I
was almost forty-six years old. I had sadly decided that
perhaps Creation would not give me my own children in this
lifetime, even though that had been the greatest wish of all
my years. So you can imagine how exciting and powerful
was the conception of our first child and the slow progress
of gestation.

Emmy and I sought the most loving and supportive
environment possible for the birth. We found that in a community, a newly-created tribe called The Farm in Tennessee.

Later Emmy would be inspired by that experience to become a midwife herself. Later still, many native women would come to The Farm to re-learn this important skill that had in many places been taken from the people, and to teach this important early step for survival and sovereignty to their own people back home.

The day of the birth, Emmy and I were in the fields picking strawberries. The closeness to the earth, the strawberries, sweet with the juice of life and sacred, the loving warmth of the good people of that tribe around us, brought us together in wonder and appreciation to the Creator for the marvel of existence and the mystery of birth. That evening we stepped outside the lodge to greet Grandmother Moon and ask her blessing. We stood quietly under the trees and clung to each other, feeling the little life throbbing and stirring in her belly, and watching the millions of stars above pulsing in the same universal rhythm. It was a moment of the greatest awe and the profoundest connection. Her contractions had begun, and the midwives had been called. Our hearts were so full it was hard to speak.

Two hours later I sat on a sleeping mat in the back room of the large tent-cabin. Emmy's head strained backwards in my lap, her face contorted, strained with an incredible energy that was moving through her and in her. She groaned and gasped in intense concentration, striving to breathe, to relax, an effort to produce non-effort, control to reduce control.

For me the world slowed and came to a stop.

There in that moment was the first time I saw her, standing by the wall of a crowded room in Phoenix, listening to the droning voice of the Indian mystic, her dark profile classically framed by her long, straight, black hair streaked with one ribbon of premature silver. Under my intense stare she turned her head slowly, raised the heavy lids of her large black eyes and returned my gaze without a smile or a flinch — only the faintest blush rising on her tawny cheeks. From there time collapsed in a heap, jumbling together mountains and deserts and thousands of miles, with joy and confusion and hurt and love, understanding only that Creation had brought us together and somehow we were supposed to make our two one: a family. And then in her womb a life from my seed that would change and determine us for the rest of our lives. Whatever might happen in our lives, our destinies were bound firmly together from that moment.

"Don't push," said Mary-Louise. The midwife's sure hands massaged the thinly stretched opening. A glistening dome of dark matted hair began to crown and bulge slowly into view. I held my breath, feeling my pulse throb in my ears.

Emmy breathed a long sigh. All energy was focused now through Mary–Louise. The candlelight glowed around her like an aura. Ruth, the assistant, was holding Emmy's hand. Donna watched beatifically from the shadows. She had given birth to five of her own.

A dark serene little face twisted through now. The mid-wife's deft fingers found the umbilicus around the neck and slipped it over the wrinkled head.

My heart seemed to pause. Eternity rushed upon me.

"Now push," said Mary–Louise, and suddenly a slippery little gray body swam into the world. The male genitalia, huge on the spindly, slimy, clay–lizard body, proclaimed the arrival of a warrior, a man child, corroborating the certainty I had since I first knew a life had been created.

Tears were streaming unnoticed down my face as I sat transfixed.

His eyes were wide open, huge and heavy–lidded like his mother's, looking about him with intense curiosity. He seemed to be noting and registering everything, without a sound. Black staring eyes and a strong high–bridged nose in a gray, impassive, meditative face. He seemed truly a being from the spirit world, a manitou, a deva, a puckwudgie, a buddha.

Mary–Louise moved him gently this way and that, examining and cleaning. Suddenly the little body flushed from gray to pink. His life became a fact to me, and I sobbed, realizing for the first time that I had been weeping since the moment I saw that serene and pensive little face.

"I wonder if he has a voice," Mary–Louise said, and I became aware of that eerie silence with which he had moved into our world, bathed in mystery. She tapped him on the bottom of his heel. He gave a short, strong "Aahh!" Not a cry. An affirmation. Everyone laughed. Emmy's arms went out, and my son settled comfortably onto his mother's breast.

I watched them together, the mother and child in their first encounter. Emmy must have been exhausted after that incredible effort, yet she glowed from within with a radiant energy. Here was the result of a year of planning and pain, of anxiety and hope, of learning and stretching, and a life-time of expectation and desire. The little face pressed into the skin of her bosom. I bathed in the light of that holy scene. The mother and child were falling in love with a feeling so ancient and deep it filled the room and illuminated every heart.

I was laughing and crying with relief and purest rapture, for the Creator had touched me, had whispered in my ear. The universe and I were one. We were babies cradled in the loving arms of the great mystery, and in some way beyond words and thoughts I understood it all at last.

Before she left us alone together with our miracle Mary-Louise asked Emmy if the man–child had a name yet.

"His name is Tokeem," said Emmy, without hesitation.

"What does that mean?"

"It means: 'I awake! I live!' "

Chapter Nine

Joyous Childraising

It is night again, and we are seated around the fire at our Watuppa Reservation. The sparks dance in the dark air and try to climb above the trees toward the stars. I have just finished telling stories, and the youngest ones are being settled down for the night in their camps.

Tomorrow I will call a children's council. I will tell some more stories then, and the young people will have a chance to discuss their own issues and tell stories. The way to really learn and understand a story is to tell it yourself, and I am hoping that some of these young ones will be able to carry on the lore of our people for the next generation. I was very proud when Tokeem, my eldest son, first stood in this circle and told one of our ancient tales to the other children, feeling this part of the Wampanoag heritage passing from the old ones through me into the future generations. Now my second son, Tashin, has begun learning and telling all the stories too.

Of all the things I want to consider in the talks we are sharing here, it is this one, about our relationship to our children, that is the closest to my heart. I have already said that my two sons are the very center of my life, but it is not only my own children that have such importance to me. Children of all ages enrich, elevate, educate me and fill me with love, hope, and gratitude.

Babies delight me, awe me, and make me feel soft and gentle and nurturing. To hold a baby in my arms connects me more than any prayer to the heart of Creation's mystery. The innocent trust of their sleep brings forth my deepest instincts of protection and caring. The curiosity of big, staring eyes and tiny, groping fists reaching into a vast, unknown world excites me with the potential of all the adventure that exists in the universe. And to have those little fingers grip my finger firmly, to see a big toothless smile light that little face, is to have my heart spring like a dolphin in sudden joy.

Toddlers reawaken my consciousness to the miracles of little ordinary things I never notice. Walking with Raven, the three-year old of our community, you can't just rush down the path to where you are going. You have to go at her pace and look at the wonders around you, the grass, the butterflies, the puddles of water. Sometimes she will squat down and just look at the ground for a long time. If you can forget your goal and your impatience for a little, you go and squat with her and enter her world. There are ants there, busy with a whole different life. And a caterpillar, and a beetle, some interesting holes in the ground, and many little stones. She picks up a stone and looks at it closely. Then, glad for your company in her exploration, she hands it to you. What a marvel is this little stone of green and blue and gray! Set in silver you would praise its beauty and perfection, but here you just stepped on it along with hundreds of other miracles, ground into the earth everywhere you walk. This little child looks at you now for your reactions. She is your teacher, sharing her special world with you, and when you smile back you are the teacher too, sharing the confidence and the love of your years of living on this earth she now wants to explore.

For two years now, Raven has been giving herself instructions in the language. Learning the words, saying them over and over, chanting them, crooning them, shouting them. And then the questions. So many questions! So much to learn to be able to care for yourself in a world of so many things, animals, and people. How fast they learn! Every day there are new words, new ideas, new accomplishments. Why, if we all kept learning new words, new ideas, new accomplishments, new skills every day at the rate we learned as infants, we should all be the greatest poets, philosophers, scientists that ever lived!

Joy comes through our contact with human beings and other creatures, with the living earth and sky, and for me, my greatest joys come through my contacts with children. Childraising has been a true joy for me since my first son was born, but I must admit I made a lot of mistakes practicing on other people's children, as a relative, a teacher, or a friend earlier in my life. Fortunately for my own children, they came late in my life after many adventures and learnings with many other children, and particularly after experiencing the childraising philosophy of traditional native people in action.

C hildren are the heart center of the family, as the family is the heart center of the community and of society. So childraising is a crucial consideration for our survival, crucial to the family, to the community and to society, crucial to the survival of our Indian nations and traditional ways.

I believe with all my heart and mind that the traditional native ways of childraising represent the only ways that human parents have discovered to relate to their children in a healthy and balanced way, consistent with the universal, spiritual principles we have been discussing.

These traditional ways were developed over a million years of tribal living experience. Not only on this continent, but all over the world, natural tribal peoples have lived and transmitted essentially the same beliefs and ways of living from generation to generation with peace and stability, equality and well–being for all members of the community. The experience of living with young people growing to adulthood within these families is, on the whole, one of relaxed enjoyment and delight. That accords with our understanding of the Original Instructions saying that children are our greatest blessing and caring for them is our greatest joy.

For one million years the traditional tribal ways have proved successful in holding together the warp and weft of human society in its natural environment. A mere few thousand years ago the ways of civilization began to rise and have already wreaked such havoc upon the earth that the future of the human species is in serious jeopardy. In the past few decades the quality of life has deteriorated rapidly, and most rapidly in the urban centers that are the very fruit and flower and seed of this civilization.

So it would seem to be in the best interest of all people, no matter what their race or heritage, to learn and adapt to the healthy and balanced old family ways.

What are these traditional ways? Looking at natural tribal groups that survive and resist assimilation in North, Central and South America, Africa, Australia and a few island societies, I would use two words to describe the basic spiritual understanding which underlies all their customs and traditions, including the raising of children.

These two words are Trust and Respect.

I n the upper Amazon region of Ecuador, the Waorani people live as their ancestors lived, a nomadic jungle life of hunting and gathering and gardening, moving their villages when the fragile garden soil gives out. Here we can see traditional childraising uninfluenced by any intrusion of modern culture. The children are happy, lively, involved with interest in all aspects of the community. There are no schools or childcare facilities. The children follow older children and adults and learn by watching and trying. Everything in the village is shared, fruit from gathering, meat from hunting, and tools. Children cooperate because this is all they see. The idea of competition is unknown to them. There is no rivalry among siblings. Children have equal rights and are loved and cared for by all adults. They are everybody's children, and they are treated with trust and complete respect.

The concept of Trust permeates all, shown by a simple faith in the laws and relationships of Creation. In terms of childrearing this means a trust in the basic goodness, intelligence and resourcefulness of children. In the "civilized" world people do not trust each other, and they do not trust their children. Children grow up in an atmosphere of mistrust. They do not trust others, and they do not trust themselves.

No wonder love is so fragile in that world. No wonder families and communities disintegrate.

Trust is not a quality that can be preached or lectured or inculcated or disciplined into a child. It can be destroyed that way but it can only be fostered by trust, by unconditional love and caring. Babies come trusting into the world, expecting to be kept safe, to be fed, to be warm, to be cuddled and loved. To keep that trust we need only keep faith with that baby's expectations. As soon as we take that baby away from its mother, we are shattering that trust. If that baby does not go on the mother's breast and feel her warmth, hear her familiar heartbeat, and suck of that milk when it is hungry, millions of years of genetic expectations are frustrated.

Let us say that this baby was born at home, or in a very enlightened hospital which gave the mother her baby as soon as it was born. Trust continues. But sometime later the baby goes in a crib. The baby wants to be held and cuddled but suddenly she is alone, looking at the world through bars. In prison already! She doesn't even know what she did wrong! She cries. Her diaper is changed, and she has been fed. Why is she crying? She gets picked up and walked about. She stops crying and falls asleep. That was it, she was tired. But why couldn't she sleep? Perhaps she needed the assurance of human contact. She gets put back in the crib. Later she wakes with a start and reaches out for momma. Nothing there. Abandoned again. Heartbroken, she wails. After what seems an eternity someone comes, and the routine repeats. Changed and fed and walked and put back in the crib. Is this living? Hey, warden, when does my parole come up?

Traditional native children are always kept in close physical contact with at first the mother, and then with other family members. The mother holds the baby while she does her work, on her lap or in a sling close to her body. When the baby goes into a cradleboard, she is snuggled warmly with a blanket and propped close where she can watch what her mother is doing. She feels in touch and safe as mother talks and sings to her and lets her know that all is well and as it should be. Trust continues.

At night the baby sleeps at her mother's side. When she wakes for a feeding she will not cry out alone in the dark, she will merely reach out for that dependable breast that is right there. In a tribal situation, if the mother is sick or incapacitated, a wet nurse will be found who can sleep with the baby. Satisfied, the baby sleeps again, her trust undisturbed.

Grandmother is there to hold her, and then an aunt, and a big sister, and the father, grandfather, uncles, brothers, as well as cousins. The baby gets passed around a lot to many friendly, affectionate arms. Trust grows.

When does the baby first experience being alone? When she grows big enough, independent and curious enough, to crawl away on her own. She will try it out just a little way and scurry back. Feeling safe, she will try it a little further and a little further, until the next thing you know she is getting married and having her own baby.

There, in a very short story, is the basic teaching of traditional native childraising. What is that teaching? Stay close, stay available, and let them be.

That is the way of trust.

What about respect? Trust is what the traditional native person feels, and respect is the way the traditional native person expresses that feeling to everything in Creation.

Most people agree that respect is a good thing. What they do not agree on is how to teach it. Respect is not taught by coercion. You cannot demand respect. If you demand it, what you will get will not be respect. It may be fear, or it may be submission, or it may be sullen, covert rebellion. But it is not respect.

Then how do you instill respect in your child? Respect, like trust, like curiosity, comes from within. If you want your child to respect others, you must show respect to your child, to your mate, to your parents, to all your relatives and friends and all their children. Respect is a personal value. Values cannot be taught by lecture, reward or punishment. They can only be taught by example.

Where values are concerned, I think of myself as a counselor to my children. I cannot force my values on them. I can only offer my thinking as a resource to them. If they are to hire me as an advisor, they must have reason to seek my advice. They must be able to see that my life works well for me and for those around me. I may offer unsolicited opinions, but only once, for information. Repetition is preaching and will not be heard.

When we love our children, when we trust and respect them, our children return that love and trust and respect. When we accept and appreciate our children for the miracles of Creation that they are, what they return is acceptance and appreciation. As surely as a wolf cub will imitate its parents, your child will model herself on you and your values.

Creation knows what it is doing. All it requires of adults is that they don't abandon their young. Children don't need a lot of instruction. In fact, they learn best when they are not taught. Creation made them imitators, and that's how they learn most efficiently. Whatever we want them to do or be we have to do or be ourselves.

Of course, eventually they will model many people. But their first models are mother and father. Then brother and sister. Maybe eventually they will want to be like Grandfather, or Aunt Ramona or old Henry next door. They probably will try a lot of models before they begin to develop their own way.

Who is their guide in this education? Creation is — which is to say, they are themselves. The impulse comes from within.

Of course, you can put stimulations around them. By your enthusiasm and love you can inspire them. But try to push it too hard and you will meet resistance. You will dampen the desire you want to kindle. Because the impulse to learn must come from within them, not from within you.

That is the way of trust. You trust that all you need to do is love that child, shelter her, feed her, protect her from physical danger, and be available for her when she needs you. Creation takes care of the rest. You don't have to preach or lecture or punish, you don't have to cajole or reward, praise or blame. All you have to do is be there for her, accept her, support her, appreciate her for who she is.

Our people understand that young people, seeking to grow strong and independent, look to sources beyond their parents. That is as it should be. In the old ways of many of our nations, there is often someone other than a parent who is responsible for the guidance of a young person. This might be an aunt or an uncle, a clan mother, clan uncle or grand-parent. Beyond the circle out of which the child seeks to grow, this person is teacher, counselor, friend, and ally. This counselor appreciates the young person for what she or he is, as an individual, beyond the reflections of family pride. These teachers prepare the young people for their initiations into adulthood and their responsibilities within the family clan, society, and nation. Their attitude towards their young disciples is one of complete respect and trust.

Perhaps the most terrible aspect of the conquest and domination of our people by the distressed culture with which we all must now contend, is the lack of understanding and appreciation of our traditional native ways. We have so much to be proud of in our heritage, and the wisdom of the old ways of childraising is one of our crowning glories.

This philosophy and way of life are so little known that very few people not raised in that tradition are aware of it. Even Indian people who are a generation or more removed from that experience no longer understand it. I notice that in today's society childraising does not seem to be a joy to most parents, but a struggle, a bewilderment, and often a frustrating exhaustion. In desperation, parents today abandon their custodial responsibilities to the seduction of an unhealthy contemporary culture, canned entertainment, chemical foods, and a cornucopia of narcotics from caffeine to crack.

Nothing makes me sadder than to visit the home of a contemporary Indian family and see the kids riveted to the television, sugared and chemicaled foods on the table, and the parents ordering the young people around and arguing with each other. It's not their fault. They are the victims of the pervasive mental and moral decay of that oppressive, dominant culture.

Of course I don't let on that I don't approve of any of what they are doing. That's not our way. All I can do is talk about these things at our ceremonies in a general way, or at lectures I am invited to make, or write articles that they may someday read. But I can tell what will happen to that family. I know that if that family is joining with others to fight for their rights as Indians, they will seek out the traditional ways. They will come to ceremonies and gatherings and listen to their elders. And when they learn of traditional childraising, they will begin to think and to change, and they will begin to come closer together.

I also know that if that family is not interested in recovering its heritage and does not seek it with all its energy, it will begin to disintegrate like the other families of the dominant culture. The generation gap will grow wide and deep. The parents will split up, the kids will leave home. Alcohol and drugs will begin to cripple some of those individuals. Some may escape and fight for their own survival alone, and sadly some may leave far behind the struggles of their own people.

That is why in our war against alcohol and drugs our traditional ways are our best resource. These ways are rooted in the family, not the isolated nuclear family, but the extended family. They are based on relationship, on closeness, on people being committed to each other, being there for each other in times of need. They are based on people helping people, on families helping each other. These traditional ways center first of all upon our children. These ways work well for children, because they provide children with a proud sense of their own worth, with trust and dignity and appreciation. Our children are our best hope for eliminating alcohol and drug abuse forever. This is the crucial struggle for us, because our children are our survival.

As the great Hunkpapa medicine man Sitting Bull has said, "Let us put our minds together and see what kind of life we can make for our children."

W hen I see people ordering their children around like slaves, getting angry and shouting if they don't measure up to the parents' standards, when I see kids being hit or bribed, I feel very sad. Those parents don't trust their children, because they have not been trusted themselves. They don't trust Creation. They don't know what trust is.

I am especially sad when I see modern Indian parents acting like this, because without realizing it they are imitating the dominant culture's destructive methods that are responsible for the dissolution of the family and the collapse of spiritual values.

That dissolution began when Indian children were taken from their homes and put in boarding schools. When they went home, they often couldn't even talk with their parents because they hadn't been allowed to speak their Indian languages at school. Thousands of years of gentle, trusting, traditional childraising were lost to many of our people who began to follow the European models.

The European traditions mistrust all of nature, and they mistrust human nature most of all. The concept of Original Sin is fundamental to European law and custom. According to that view human beings are naturally corrupt, greedy, aggressive, sybaritic and self–indulgent, and their anti–social passions can only be restrained under the threat of punishment or promise of reward.

The fact is, good and bad are social concepts and are meaningless when applied to a newborn infant. A baby is not greedy or corrupt or lazy — neither is it generous or noble.

A baby may be hungry. A baby may be curious. A baby may be tired and confused or energetic and expansive. But a baby has no concept of power, although it may feel frustrated if it is restrained. A baby has no concept of ownership, but will be outraged if you take away something it has a grip on.

Little human beings, besides being fed, kept warm and dry and assured of having safe, familiar care available to them, need to expand and explore. The most important thing about our species comes to the fore early in life. Human beings are endlessly curious. They need to explore themselves and their environment.

It is a real need. When a baby is not allowed to explore, when it is placed in a crib or playpen, when it is told "no–no" to everything it wants to touch, it becomes exasperated and puts out more energy, crying, trying to grab. The adult gets more forceful. Look at it from the baby's view. There's someone ten times bigger than you frustrating your every move. What kind of a world is this, anyway?

A better move is to baby–proof the environment and let the child have some scope. This means putting everything dangerous or really valuable out of the way. But don't go too far and remove all possible interests and stimulations, or you will turn the whole house into a barren jail, in which case baby loses interest. The searching brain is confronted with nothing to learn, and she is craving to learn, every minute of her waking life. With no stimulation the child becomes bored and slows down. Later on people will call her stupid. She started out as intelligent as anyone, with a whole universe of potentiality before her. Her body was fed, but not her mind, and so it atrophied, withered from lack of use.

When a person's natural curiosity is allowed full play, learning takes place at an amazing rate. Look at how quickly everyone learns to speak. The more talking the child hears in her home, the faster she learns. But if someone tried to teach a baby to talk with lectures and exercises and homework, if the methods we use to teach writing or arithmetic or history in school were used to teach talking, it would take the child years to learn to speak, and then probably with difficulty.

When someone tells you, "Learn this!" you will have no curiosity about it at all. You will work to learn it if you have to, but your heart won't be in it. Your curiosity comes from inside you as a response to something interesting in your environment — as long as it's not forced on you. When your curiosity is aroused, it gives you a lot of energy. You won't stop until you have learned all you can to satisfy that curiosity, and in the process you'll get curious about something else.

That's how Creation works. Nourished by love and acceptance, encouraged by the availability of grown–up allies, and strengthened by curiosity, children grow into powerful and creative adults who will give the same nurture and appreciation to their children. That is the way of trust.

But what of conflicts? Whenever people live together, as in a family, conflicts arise from time to time. Does the traditional native parent just let the child have her own way all the time, even at the expense of the rest of the family?

Here again the guides are respect and trust. The person in the parenting or teaching role allows the child full independence and autonomy. The child will be allowed to find her own way and make her own mistakes. The child will always know, however, that some responsible adult is available for advice and assistance whenever the child may seek it. Help is neither offered nor withheld, but it is always available.

If what the child wants unavoidably conflicts with the needs or wishes of the parent, they will seek a solution together in an atmosphere of mutual respect. This feeling of respect is so high in a traditional native home that no child would conflict with what that child knew to be of great importance to an elder. And no elder would stand in the way of what the elder knew to be of great importance to a child, for what is important to the child provides the learning and growth that will one day sustain the people and the nation. In such an atmosphere, conflict is very rare and solutions are not difficult to find.

Now, those statements sound too ideal by a lot, I know, and I need to say a few more things to give a little life and reality to that picture. The picture is, in the whole, a true one, as I have observed it in homes of traditional Indian families throughout North America. I should also say that this is true to the degree that that family is remote from the pressures of the dominant culture of the country, be it Anglo or Latino. In the context of traditional spiritual trust and respect, there is a gentleness, a warm, humorous, and relaxed quality that is a world apart from the tensions and conflicts of the average "civilized" home, be it rich or poor, middle class or working class, suburban or rural.

T he dominant culture gives only lip-service to children. Parents are isolated and given no assistance, but are told they are responsible for the care and for the behavior of their children. Parents are afraid to take their children anywhere — they are not wanted in most places. They have no place where the parents work; where children are tolerated, there are severe restrictions on them. Going to some place to work is described as having a career, but taking care of a home and children is not. In a culture that places its values on the amount of recompense, childcare and teaching are underpaid and undervalued, and parenting is unpaid and unvalued. Parents are the last oppressed group to recognize their own oppression and to struggle for their liberation, largely because they are so isolated.

The young people of today are also an oppressed group. The oppression is enforced in families and schools by denial of any respectful attention, invalidation of their thinking and feelings, misinformation, physical abuse, negative attitudes and low expectations, and economic dependency. Young people have few rights beyond that of freedom from physical battering. Their space and their persons are not respected. They are not paid just compensation for their labor. They are not listened to. Their feelings are not considered important. They are not prized, appreciated, and encouraged in what they do. As babies, though they are constrained, they are thought cute and lovable. But the older they get, the less they are cherished, honored, and treasured for the wonderful human beings they are.

This oppression of young people keeps all of society from the advantages of youthful clear thinking and high hopes for the world. Young people are naturally loving, intelligent, creative and full of fun when they are free of the dismal conditioning of society's institutions. Since young people are half of the world's population, with the encouragement and support of the rest of us, in a short time they could change the world into a more joyous and human place for us all.

In the supportive environment of a community based upon the sacred circle, a community in which the rearing, the care and education of children is shared by aunts and uncles, grandparents, older siblings and cousins, clan members and the community as a whole, there is not a lot of time and attention required from a parent or from any one person. But until we have been able to recreate our communities as sacred circles, it would help if each one of us would give some extra thought and a little more of our time and attention to the children around us. They are indeed all our children after all. And there is much that one person can do which can be of memorable importance in the life of a child.

How can we be better allies for parents and for young people today? I think this is the important question. We can be better allies for parents if we can take some time to give them attention. Parents and non–parents need to understand the oppressive conditions of parenting and join together to support each other and share childcare. We can play with young people more, take more interest in their interests, follow their leadership and initiative.

We can honor their feelings and encourage their expression. There are so many ways adults deny the expressions of children's feelings. When they are angry, we tell them to be "nice." When they are sad, we tell them to cheer up, everything is all right. When they are afraid, we tell them there's nothing to be afraid of. Adults don't like feeling those feelings, so they deny them in their children. They don't realize that the expression of the feeling is not the hurt but the healing of the hurt.

Probably your own childhood was not exactly as you would have wished. Probably you were not always respected and cherished by the adults around you. This is true to some extent for all of us. But now we have a chance to make a big difference in the lives of children and in the future of the world.

We can offer to all young people of any age complete respect as a full human being. We can value them as unique, independent creatures with ideas and desires of their own. It is important for young people to have one person who respects them, who has no prior expectations about what the shape and form of their lives should be, who applauds them for trying out new things, who doesn't get upset when they are distressed, who knows that their distress is not who they are.

Children come into the world joyously, expecting it to be fun, expecting us to be fun, and to play with them. But we have grown old and serious. Children can teach us to be joyous again. Children are excited to be alive, and they need to see people who are as excited about their being alive as they are.

Let us try our magic feather again. Take hold of it with me now, and we will be transported to a traditional community that lies far from here. It is familiar to me, yet it is not any single community but a composite of many, and the family we visit is a composite of many traditional families I have known, from Akwesasne in New York to Third Mesa in Arizona, from Alaska to Guatemala.

There is a ceremony in the village today, and many relatives have gathered for the occasion. As a result there is a larger herd of children than usual running together in the road and across the field. They run to us as we approach and surround us. Their eyes are merry as they boldly ask us who and what we are, and they giggle at our answers. This is not mockery or malicious laughter, but simple joy at a surprising and endlessly funny world.

Now they have cleverly wormed it out of me that I am a storyteller, and they won't let us escape without a story. After one story, I notice that the crowd of children sitting around listening intently has more than doubled as mysteriously the news of storytelling has spread like a net and drawn in every last child in the village. These are children who are used to storytelling and listen with rapt concentration.

As we finish, we walk into the village surrounded by a great horde of shouting, laughing children. Some call out the news of who and what we are to any within earshot. Others delegate themselves to run home and tell their families. Soon invitations are coming from all sides, borne back by little emissaries from their parents. We accept the first invitation and follow a pack of a half–dozen assorted siblings to their small, family house.

The father greets us outside with a big glad–to–see–you

grin and ushers us in. Another gracious smile from the mother inside welcomes us. She gestures at the table, the father speaks a couple of words in the Indian language, and the children bring up chairs for us to sit, bring bowls of stew from the mother at the stove, and stand around to encourage us to eat. The stew is as comforting and nourishing as the atmosphere of this generous and friendly home.

Soon relatives begin to come in and out the door. All greet us. Some sit with us at the table and are immediately given a bowl of stew. The invariable custom in any Indian home is: greet the guests and feed them right away. People begin to coalesce into groups: women with women, men with men, children running in and out. Faces appear and disappear at the doors and windows. Yet the atmosphere is not one of noise and confusion, but relaxed and easy-going. Conversations are quiet and slow, punctuated with little bursts of laughter. Work is being done, jobs being taken without assignment or organization.

Soon we all are on our way to the ceremonies. Several children explain to us what will happen, what we will see, what the songs and the dances and the games will be and what they mean. The children all dance. As soon as they can toddle they begin to imitate the others, hopping and stomping. Then the elders speak. Long speeches in the Indian language. Everyone listens quietly, including the older children who have begun to understand the importance of these ways and the greatness of this heritage. The little children run around the outside of the circle or climb on family laps. Between the speeches there is a lingering silence as the words of the speaker sink quietly into the minds of the listeners, into their feeling places, into the grass and stones, into the soil of the earth, and then spread away like the thinning smoke of the fire onto the winds of the universe.

Following there is a feast. Everyone has had some hand in it, preparing food or building fires or cutting wood, and this is the culmination of all that community activity. The children are brought to a separate table and served — reminding us that we are here to serve Creation's future. The old people sit and are served. Everyone else gets in line. There is a lot of good food and lots of joking. It is another good day, as it has been for thousands of years among our people.

Our new friends have invited us to stay on and spend the night, and we accept. At home the children of the family ask for a story again, but we say we'd like to hear some of their stories now. The oldest child tells a favorite story, looking to grandfather now and then, who corroborates with a nod and a grunt. Then grandfather tells a story and asks me if we have a story like that. Then I tell one of our stories on a similar theme, and so the evening goes until one by one people grow tired and withdraw for the night. Sleeping children are carried away to bed, and we are left alone.

It has been a slow and easy day despite the excitements of visitors and ceremonies. Nothing pressed or rushed, everything proceeding at a comfortable pace with plenty of time for joking and playing. There's no hurry. Stepping out of the goals and schedules of civilization, we are back in a world without time. The earth, the sun and the stars are not in a race. The life of the people is ageless, and every moment is a perfect eternity.

And what of the children of this family? They seem to live more in the adult world than the children of the dominant culture. They have no special playroom or playground (and in the oldest, most isolated communities they would have no schoolhouse). The world is not separated into adult's and child's. The child learns and finds her way in a unified world, her people's world. There are not great varieties of toys. The implements of play are found in the world, except for a few toys made by the child or by a relative: a doll, a small bow and arrows. Mostly the toys are real tools, growing in size as the child grows. These few objects of play and learning are more prized and appreciated by traditional native children, more cared for and more used than other children's closetsful of manufactured toys that have been purchased from vast retail emporiums upon the overloaded hawking of advertisements and now lie broken or abandoned in favor of some newer interest.

Most of all, these children are not treated in a special way reserved only for children, except in concerns for their feeding and safety. They are full people treated with the respect due to persons of all ages. All day we have not heard the special language and tone we hear addressed to children in the dominant culture: no baby talk, no ordering around, no shouting, coaxing, wheedling, no bribery, sarcasm or demeaning put–downs. Correction of mistakes or dangerous behavior comes gently, casually, with no blame or tension, from whomever is near, older brother or sister, grandmother, uncle, friend. No conflicting relationships have been established. Father has no expectations, makes no demands, so there is no need for separation, rebellion. Father and mother trust their children will learn and figure out the world for themselves, and become the best of what they can be if they are allowed to find their own way.

That is respect. And trust.

These children are not as loud and explosive as children of the dominant culture because they do not have to fight an oppressive system. They do not have to let off steam after being suppressed at desks and forced to pay attention to uninteresting things for precious hours of their young lives while outside the windows important things are happening: chickadees are playing, the arbutus is peeping up through the snow, and all over the civilized world teachers are describing the conquests of Julius Caesar to kids who are learning only that the world is a crazy place, and the things adults value are really dumb.

There are no professional teachers in this traditional village and no professional babysitters. Everyone is available to the children as a resource of knowledge, as an ally and helper, as a protector. No one has to get paid to keep the children out of everyone's way in their own special world. The kids are living and growing in the world with everyone else.

If the children get too loud or wild, the request for consideration comes with the same respect that one would use for the same request of an adult. Adults understand that children tend to be more energetic and more experimental than adults and are in general more tolerant and indulgent than adults of the dominant culture. It is not that they love their children more, but only that their love is expressed through a long tradition of respect and trust. They know babies love to bang pots and scatter them all over the floor and that, while noisy and messy, the benefit to the child is far greater than the small inconvenience to the adult, so they allow them this great pleasure.

They don't worry over their health and safety obsessively, by insisting that they eat and drink in certain ways, or forbidding access to places of imagined danger. Adults in this traditional village trust that as soon as children can feed themselves they will eat as much as they need. They trust that as soon as children can dress themselves they will quickly learn how much to wear to keep warm and dry.

They trust, and thousands of years of living has borne out this trust, that children are naturally intelligent enough and resourceful enough that, once apprised of the danger, they will not burn themselves on stoves, stab themselves with knives, or do any of the things dominant culture parents imagine and worry about constantly.

Traditional Indian kids don't do any of those things. They

are smarter and more responsible than that. Because people aren't always telling them what to do and what not to do, they figure things out a lot earlier and become more self-reliant at a younger age than most children in society today.

Because becoming responsible is a mark of growing up, they follow the ways of other children a year or so older. In this way, when the time comes, children learn jobs that fit into the life and work of the family and of the community.

That's why today we didn't see a lot of organizing. Suggestions are made to children in a friendly way. If the child does not respond, she probably isn't old enough. If he is old enough, perhaps a parent may talk to him, still in a respectful, trusting way. If there is the slightest feeling by the child of oppression, then it will be better if grandfather, or an uncle, or older brother or a friend should talk to him. Someone that he trusts has no oppressive intention, no program or expectations, and speaks only from friendship can sometimes make suggestions more easily.

These ways can still be found in the remote areas, away from civilization. In many places civilization is moving closer, claiming the children for its schools, luring the families (impoverished by the theft of their land and resources) into the cities and the ranks of unemployment and welfare. In those places it's hard to live the old ways. It's not that these traditional values cannot be maintained in a family that has a lot of contact with the dominant culture, but such a family must be more conscious of the threats to its values and more zealous in protecting them.

One such family I have known is that of Janet and the late Don McCloud in the Puyallup and Nisqually area of Washington State. This family has been engaged in the struggle for their people's rights, including fishing rights, since the early sixties, aided by such allies as Dick Gregory and Marlon Brando, as well as native leaders and warriors from many nations. Being the focus of so much tension and attention has naturally been a burden at times. Because of their continued espousal of traditional spiritual values, and the help of Indian spiritual leaders from all over Turtle Island, and due to the acute intelligence and fiery stamina of Janet, and the gentle, good-humored strength of Don, they became an example to all of endurance under tremendous pressure. It is a great fortune and strength for my family here in the East to have known and been inspired by these good friends of the West for so many years, and it was a great privilege for me to have performed a traditional wedding ceremony for two of their daughters.

Barbara, Janet's youngest daughter, has now grown to leadership in her people's interests and edits a journal for Northwest native women. When she was quite a young girl she illustrated in an unexpected way to me the respect taught in that family. At the United Nations Habitat conference in Vancouver, British Columbia, we had an Indian spiritual gathering convened by a number of traditional Hopi elders who had caravanned from Arizona. Our friend Thomas Banyacya had a statement from the elders which he hoped to deliver at a meeting in the Queen Elizabeth Theatre. The Indians all went to listen, but we were not allowed entrance to the hall. The management seemed to be afraid of so many Indians, even though we said we were a peaceful spiritual gathering. They decided to let a few people in, one at a time, and many non-Indians, used to protests and occupations, crowded to the entrance. The Indians mostly stayed back and watched.

The exception was my young friend Barbara McCloud. Being small, she slipped and squirmed unnoticed through the crowd jam until she was in front of the door. When it was her turn to go in she stood fast, refusing to enter and not letting anyone else go in past her.

I didn't notice this at first. All I could tell from where I was behind the crowd was that there was some commotion. Then someone passed the message that the door guards wanted me to go up there, and the crowd opened a grudging path for me. I thought they wanted me to arbitrate some dispute, and I was surprised to find that it was little Barbara blocking the door.

"Would you please go in, sir?" the guard pleaded, "This little girl says she won't go in until her elder goes in."

I looked at Barbara. She glowed with quiet inner strength as she regarded the guard with a resolute stubbornness, but there was a hint of a conspiratorial smile as she glanced at me. We shared a deep, ancient secret and a power.

I took her arm, and we went in together.

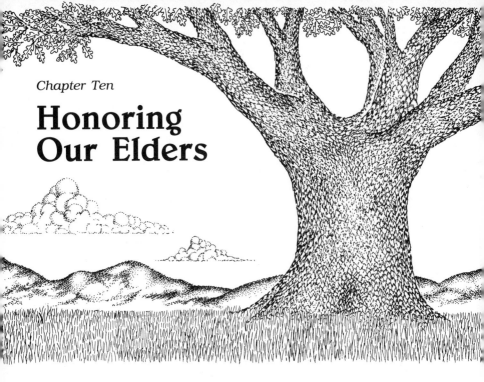

Chapter Ten

Honoring Our Elders

Come with me down this country lane to a field by a wood behind the old meeting house in Dighton.

That solitary tree there in the meadow, reaching five large long branches outward like fingers of a huge hand trying to grasp the sky, that great oak is very ancient and sacred to our people. It is known as the Council Oak, and it was a mature tree three and a half centuries ago. The great sachems of those times, Ousemequin, Wamsutta, and Metacomet, used to gather the sachems and elders of Pokonoket here to council on matters affecting the nation.

Look up from underneath and see how the tree creates its own world beneath it. If you stay here quietly for a while, away from the noises of the road and the doings of people, if you stay with the soft song of the wind in its leaves, perhaps it may speak to you, as it has often done to me. It has seen much and heard much, this old tree. I am grateful to it for surviving, for growing so old and being there for us. Here we touch our history and the experience of a thousand winters and summers.

That is why some of our people organized a powwow in this town a few years ago, to let the people of the town know how important the tree is. There had been plans for development that would have destroyed the tree. Now the town has taken an interest in the tree and it is being protected. That is good. Every year now they have this powwow, and some of *us elders take a little trip at sunrise to have a ceremony here at the tree.*

The experience of age is a great gift to a family, a tribe, and a nation. I am so glad to see these elders coming to our gatherings still — in their eighties, nineties, even over a hundred years old. It gives strength to us as a people. Our councils of elders are a sharing of wisdom and knowledge that benefits all the people. Nothing makes our people happier than to see the little ones and the old ones when we all come together.

In most of the traditional communities I have visited, when there is a feast the little ones and the elders are served before the adults from youth to middle age. That indicates our priorities. The little ones are our survival in the future. The elders are our link to the past, our heritage, the tribal wisdom. If there should not be enough food in hard times, the adults could withstand the privation better than the very young and the very old.

The strength and the very identity of a community, of a tribal band, is indicated by the way it treats its children and its elders.

My grandfather used to take me to visit the burial grounds of our people — he knew of many of them throughout Pokonoket country, on the Cape and the islands, and there was one right next to where we lived, where the chief Mashantampaine was buried. Nowadays there is so much construction going on that we have to be on our guard that these sacred places are not disturbed. Sometimes they are accidentally discovered, and we have to go and recover those remains and rebury them in a good way. Even so, many of the things our old ones took into the earth with them, and sometimes even the bones of our ancestors themselves, find their way into museums. Then we try to get them back, but people do not always understand our point of view. They think whatever is lying in the ground is free for anyone to take. Sometimes if we suggest that we might go and dig up their honored dead in Arlington they begin to see our point. My brother Slow Turtle, supreme medicine man of our nation, works continually to protect our Ancestors' graves.

The way that the old people were buried with their own things, the care that was taken, shows that in those most ancient times of the people, there was a sacred circle, a community, and the community honored its elders.

If a community has no elders, it does not know who or what it is. If a community does not respect its elders, it does not care who or what it is. Like a person, a community needs to have an identity. To be strong and healthy it must know and like itself. A community that does not know and love its elders cannot know itself. A community that does not honor and revere its elders cannot like itself.

There is a natural link between the children and the elders. Elders are the nicest thing that could happen to children. Children are the elders' greatest joy.

Can you remember how wonderful it was to spend time with your favorite grandparent when you were a child? Elders are not too busy to spend time with the young ones, to give them good attention and appreciation, to listen to them, encourage them, take pride in their creations and successes.

Little children need to be held and fondled. Most people are too busy during the day, but elders have time and love to spend on little ones. We older folks get to re-live our childhood in the excitement and enthusiasm of the young. Our laps are available for climbing onto, our arms are free for holding, our faces and noses are the most interesting things for pulling and poking.

As children grow, they love stories. And who has all the interesting stories? And who loves to tell them, loves a fascinated new audience? We do. The elders. The people who have spent a lifetime living, hearing and watching stories unfold.

My father's father had the time to take me places, to show me the old village and camp sites of our people. He showed me the old artifacts he found and told me how they were used. He had a whole attic full of them. We would stand in an old camp site or burial ground, and he would tell me about those who had lived and died there. He would tell me to think about them and honor them. Then we would just stand quietly. I would hear the winds in the trees, the rustle of birds in the leaves. Then a feeling began to come over me. I could feel the land, almost hear it speak. And I could feel the presence of all those who had lived there. It was as though men, women, old people, even little children who had only lived a brief time were whispering to me. They wanted me to be glad I was alive and also be glad that they had lived, not to forget them. They were my people. I never forgot that. They belonged to this land, and I belonged to them and to the land.

My grandfather told me stories every night. I would climb in his lap and listen, watching the gold in his teeth flash as he talked. He told me the old legends, the tales of the early times, of Maushop, Matahdou, Hobomoko, stories of Granny Squannit, Weetucks, the winds, the thunders, and the animals. The creatures of the forest and the sea all became my friends through Grandfather's stories. I became intimate with the wolf, totem of our people, the fox, the hare, the beaver, the otter, the bear, the deer, the skunk, the woodchuck, the raccoon, the turtle and the porcupine. Snakes and wildcats and mountain lions were not fearsome, only different members of our family with different customs. In the old stories all the animals and the people spoke one language. Now I had to learn anew the language of the blue jays and the crows, the gulls and the terns, the hawks and the wild geese, the robins and the doves. I lived with the herring and the perch, the cod and the mackerel, the porpoise and the shark. I felt the power of those distant mysterious beings: the moose, the eagles, and the whales.

My grandfather told me the history of our people and gave me pride in being one of them. I knew the people had always done their best, and that I would too.

My grandfather was gentle and considerate and courteous with both friend and stranger. He gave me, a young boy seeking to learn the way how to be in the world, an image of manhood, of what it is to be a man of our people. He was always generous and hospitable. He was a quiet man, interested in the world around him, its past and present. Things, people, incidents amused him easily, and he chuckled a lot with good-natured humor.

My mother's grandparents, my great-grandmother and great-grandfather, lived around the corner from the house in which I was born and lived my early years. I used to run over there every day when I was little. My great-grandfather died when I was about three or four, and I remember him only dimly. But I still can feel the warm loving quality of their relationship that had grown in love over a whole lifetime. When I see all the people having such a hard time these days keeping their relationships together, I recall the glow that filled their small, sunny rooms. They were simple people, poor people as wealth is counted in this country, but they had enough. They were rich in kindness and generosity towards each other as well as towards others. They were tolerant, patient and even-tempered. I don't know if they were always like that, or if it took a lifetime to get to that peace and understanding, but it was a good model for me. The love that filled their house felt good to a little boy making his daily rounds.

Next door to me lived an old lady who was always de-
lighted to see me, and so of course I always stopped there to
spend some of my day. As at my great–grandmother's, I
generally got oatmeal cookies and a cup of hot chocolate
there. Perhaps that's why I still like them for my favorite
treat. She was a widow who lived alone, and we had much
to give each other. For many years after I had grown older
and moved away from that town I wrote to her, and she
answered me until she died. Old people were really my best
friends when I was small.

But where are the elders in society today? They have gone
away to St. Petersburg or Sun City. They are in nursing
homes or retirement communities. They don't like children in
those places. That is too bad, for both the children and the
elders. Do you know where your elders are tonight?

The culture of western civilization today is a
youth–oriented culture. It is ageist. That is, it discriminates
against elders as a class. It gives a certain amount of
lip–service to "senior citizens" but contrives to make life more
difficult for them. People are forced into retirement at a
certain age, whether they are healthy and productive or not.
Often they accept this because of the propaganda that retirement is a reward, or because they have been told they must
move over to make room for the young people. Often people
would appreciate changing work when they get older, just for
the interest, the variety, to learn and grow and do something
different, but there are no opportunities for people of that
age. So there is an enforced idleness which creates isolation,
a loss of self–esteem, a lowering of income. Elders get the
message that they are a problem, a burden to society.

The culture in general promotes the attitudes that old
people are dependent, frail, decrepit, sick, senile,
out–of–touch, childish, or at best dull, boring, sexless,
absent–minded and dwelling in the past. It is especially
severe for women. Men are sometimes thought to be more
attractive as they grow older (up to a point), with the reverse
true for women. The whole concentration of the fashion and
cosmetics industries is upon youth, upon creating the ap-
pearance of youthfulness. With most of society having these
attitudes, old people become isolated and cut off from companionship with different age groups.

The reality is that older people are healthier now than in
the past and growing more healthy with better knowledge
and care. Their minds are sharp and more creative than
ever. They can feel more free of having to keep up appear-

ances, be free of pretense and sham. They are under less stress and pressure to succeed, and they are more patient. Generally, they have experienced more of everything than younger members of the population, including successes and failures, joys and sorrows, and especially the deaths of loved ones.

With the kind of neglect and disrespect that older people receive in modern society in general, it is small wonder that they often seek retirement communities and the company of other elders. They can at least give each other the attention they deserve and treat each other with dignity. They do not seek retreat from the little children, but often the older children who have learned disrespect and even dislike of old people from their own parents and their parents' peers are uncomfortable with elders. These generation gaps are taking their toll.

With all of this there is, naturally, a fear of aging in the general population. People don't want to be thought of as a burden, as weak, helpless, just sitting around waiting for death instead of living life to the fullest. Having entered this age of elderhood myself, I have begun to think more about this condition. I like growing older, I hope I never stop. I notice I can't punish my body as much as I did when I was younger. I have to watch how I try to compete with younger people at sports. I try to be smarter and use my energy more efficiently. I get stiffer more easily, and things take longer to heal. But I'm not afraid to involve myself, and I am dedicated to having more fun than ever in my life.

As elders we need to confront our fears of aging, sickness and death, and to contradict our feelings of fear and grief with creative activity and a new relish in the excitement of living each moment vigorously. It would certainly help if society did not cut us off from meaningful and constructive work, and did value us and our contributions.

How can you be an ally for elders? First, understand ageism. Like all prejudice it is founded on stereotyping. Realize that elders are individuals, and relate to each one as the special individual she or he is. Reach out to them. Isolation is no fun for any human being. Elders do not want to relate only to elders. Get close to an elder. Her life will be richer, and your life will be richer.

Realize that elders need touch as much as people of any age, and that it is often harder for them to get it. Affection expressed in a touch is healing and need have no sexual connotation (another problem that this society has). But realize too that sex is just as healthy and good for the old as for the young. Sexism is also at work here, because this society thinks it is all right for an older man to get close to a young woman, but has a double standard about older women getting close to young men.

I used to think it a compliment when someone was surprised at finding out how old I was, that after forty I was always thought to be ten or fifteen or even twenty years younger than I was. Talking with other elders made me realize that competing to seem youthful was a way of devaluating my age, of devaluating aging for all of us. Being tired and weak and unattractive is not a part of aging. One can be physically fit and have a trim and mobile body at any age. It is natural at any age to be supple, energetic, lively and joyful, and more and more people are aging and keeping fit. Now when a young person compliments me on my youth, I tell her gently that I am proud of my age, but accept her praise of my vigor and dedication to life and health.

Realize that any long life is a victory for everyone. Encourage older persons to be proud of themselves, as individuals, for having survived, for having the experiences they can share with others. Bring them home. Bring your families together. Enrich your communities and the lives of your children with the experience of these old ones.

Society as a whole is aging. More people are living longer and healthier and stronger than ever before, and this will continue to increase. There will be more and more elders, and we need to think well about using this valuable resource and about treating our elders much better than this society now treats them.

Suggest a council of elders for your community, not to give directives, but to share with the community the benefits of their combined knowledge and thinking. There are many problems our communities face: housing, pollution, illiteracy, crime, drug abuse, violence against women, children and elders to name a few. Our communities would do well to utilize the precious love, intelligence and energy of these honored elders in seeking solutions to these problems.

In our Indian communities the elders are still with us. We honor the long lives they have led, the service they have given to the community, to their families, to their children and grandchildren and great–grandchildren. Their experience and their wisdom are important to us. They carry our traditions and our stories.

In our new, made-up tribal community of Mettanokit, founded mostly by relatively young people, we are trying to fill in that generation gap. We have weekends when we all invite our parents to come and share a family celebration with us. It is not easy, because of that gap. We have developed a very different style of living from that of many of our parents, a style of voluntary simplicity. To some of our parents it must seem like a rebuff to their values, to all their sacrifices and hopes for our material wealth. But we try to make them as comfortable as we can, and we show them we are happy in our ways. Our little ones get the experience of grandparents all together as it was in the old tribal communities, and now one set of grandparents is talking about building a house on our land and coming to live here. That would be wonderful!

We would like to have more of these times when our older people can be with us in harmony. We would like to have more comfortable places in our growing tribal village for our children's grandparents to live among us. We do not expect too much too quickly. It is not easy to re-create a tribal village from people who have no experience of tribal living for many generations. We must be patient, but keep our minds on our vision and ever seek new ways to manifest it.

One of the things which I would like to do in our new tribal villages when they are sufficiently established, is to take into the community older people who would otherwise have to be in institutions. There are many people in nursing homes and old peoples' homes who would like to live in a tribal community, with little children to climb on their laps and to ask to hear their stories. The style of simple living and sharing makes it possible for us to accommodate a number of people who are no longer productive by society's standards. They can be, in fact, more productive and more creative as they grow older. Even when they require more care, these elders have a great deal more to offer us and our children than we could buy anywhere with the resources it takes to care for them.

If we value Creation's great gift of life and its great school of experience, then we should greatly value and honor those among us who have seen and experienced the most of life. Every individual of every age has special knowledge that we can benefit from. All deserve to be heard and appreciated.

The little children have special wisdom that we have forgotten. If we pay attention to them we can remember how it was for us when we were still so close to Creation. But the elders have special knowledge that we cannot know until we have lived their years. Their experience should be appreciated, and they should be greatly honored for just being strong and wise enough to survive.

The communities that still live in that way around the world are the communities that are strong and will endure. If we are to rebuild our communities and our society around them, we must not segregate our elders, but bring them back to strengthen our families. We must give them the respect and dignity they deserve. We must give them back to our children.

That is why our people say, "Honor the elders."

Chapter Eleven

The Daughters of Creation

This is Sakonnet Point, one of the long fingers of land that extends out into the sea from around the deep-cut bays of our Pokonoket country. There is a soft, gray fog enshrouding us here now that seems to wrap us in a blanket of light and timelessness.

There is a mystery enclosed in the name Sakonnet and in this place. Sakonnet is very close to Squawannit, which is the name of the spirit of all females. There is a variation of that in the names of Granny Squannit, an elvish magic figure of our legends, and of Squant, the wife of Maushop. In some versions of the Maushop tales, he throws his wife into the heavens before he himself leaves for another world far beyond the eastern horizon. Squant was said to have come down again at the point of Sakonnet, where she remained singing and beckoning to mariners. In historic times there was a rock that was supposed to have been Squant, and some of our people said that her arms had been broken off by English sailors.

However that may be, it is a good place for us to speak of the power and the place of women, because it was here that Awashonks, one of our most powerful women sachems, led her people in the time of Metacomet.

What we are talking about is how to live. We are talking

about how to create our own lives, and how to create our own society. We want to know what will give us the most rewarding, the most fulfilling, the most abundant and joyful lives possible.

In order to do this I look in four directions. I look back to the past to see how others have lived, especially the old ones that are our forebears on this continent. I look around at societies of human beings today for what is healthy and what is destructive. I look within myself to see what makes me feel sad or angry or confused and what makes me feel free and happy, what gives me energy and inspiration. Then I look forward to what could be, wondering how I can move along a path of Beauty in harmony with Creation.

I would like to consider now the place and power of women in the traditional tribal community. I want you to understand that I speak only with the understanding of a man. But in the sweat ceremony I sit in the west, with the women on my right and the men on my left, and as I sit there at the point of balance, feeling female energy on one side and male energy on the other, often I feel neither as man nor as woman myself. Often I feel like the rocks, receiving, absorbing the pain and bewilderment of men and women with the grace of the water. I summon that feeling to me now, to speak of women and men from that point of balance.

In the heart of our ancient teachings is the wisdom that woman is central to the creation and sustenance of life. Life arose deep in the womb of Grandmother Ocean. Our bodies come from Mother Earth, who nurtures us, shelters us, clothes us, heals us, and at the last, embraces and receives us back to the source of life. Grandmother Moon provides cycles of fertility, of planting and reaping, of cleansing and changing. Second Mother Corn, with her sisters Beans and Squash, has fed and sustained our people for thousands of summers.

All of these move, like Creation itself, in a wheel of birth, growth, maturity, decline, death and rebirth. Human females flow in this same rhythm as an extension of the universal Spirit Mother. Within the womb of every woman move the cycles that have conceived and nurtured life and ensured the continuation of the race.

As the daughters of Creation, moving in the cycles of nature and bringing forth that precious mystery of life, women are, when allowed by society and circumstance, deeply grounded in the spirit of earth and the essential. Such women are deeply religious and reverent, and profoundly thankful for the abundant gifts of Creation.

Because of their inner instinctive wisdom, women are the best guides and teachers about the preservation and sustenance of the species. One might suppose that a rational and healthy society would honor and empower their female members with enthusiasm. In the dominant cultures of today we find women demeaned, degraded, condescended to, trivialized, and exploited. It is another proof, if one were needed, that this civilization is neither rational nor healthy.

Tribal societies, on the whole, were far wiser in this respect than societies are today. Whether the people were wanderers or settled hunters, fisherfolk or farmers, they lived close to the cycles of nature. As they honored the earth, so they honored the daughters of the earth.

As I have said, tribal ways differed greatly among the native nations of North America. Among all of them, however, the women had almost total power and control within the home. Usually they owned the lodge; often they built it. The amount of influence women had in the band or village varied among different nations from direct and equal to men, to less direct but no less powerful.

The women of my people, the Wampanoag, were very powerful, and they continue to be so to this day. Squaw sachems, women leaders, were common among our bands. Weetamoo, sachem of the Pocasset tribe, reported to have been very feminine and attractive, had five husbands at various times, but it was she alone who was the sachem. She was a fierce and loyal warrior who led her band to stand by her brother Metacomet against the English. She drowned escaping from the final defeat, and the pious Pilgrims displayed her head on a pole in Plymouth town. Awashonks, the squaw sachem of this place, Sakonnet, did not marry but had many lovers, perhaps including Colonel Benjamin Church who defeated Metacomet.

Traditionally both women and children took part in the circles and councils of our people. It was felt that where elders are wise they will hear the wisdom of the young, and where men are sincere they will seek the counsel of the women.

As among most native peoples, our men and women had clearly defined roles, and as among most of the other nations of this continent, there was no shame or stigma if an individual were to choose other than a conventional role. There were, not often but occasionally, women who became hunters or warriors. Generally they dressed and lived as men and were fully accepted by other men. They were termed "man–acting" or "manly–hearted" women. Some of these would even marry women and set up regular households. Woman Chief of the Crow had several wives, befitting her position as a great warrior and chief. There were also men who dressed as women, stayed home to cook and care for the lodge and the children of other women. All of these were regarded as more than just different – they were special, even wonderful, perhaps sacred, and an object of pride to the village.

Our women had more independence than European women. They were more self–reliant and more secure. If they were unmarried they could accept or reject any man as a bed companion. Such advances were as easily made by the woman as by the man. Rape was not known to our people. Women were powerful and free and sexual relations were natural and without shame. Our people understood some ways of preventing pregnancy. For an unmarried woman to become pregnant was not desirable, but it was not a disgrace either. Women could avail themselves of the medicine woman's art of undoing pregnancy with herbs, but most would rather have the baby, since they would not be alone in that relationship. The child that might come would be loved and raised by the other women of the mother's family and clan, and by uncles and clan uncles and grandfathers too.

Almost all women and men expected to marry and to have children. There were very few spinsters or bachelors. Marriage was usually assumed to be permanent, but it could easily be dissolved by either the man or woman simply moving out – or in the case of a woman in her own house, by putting her husband's belongings out of the house. In spite of that, divorce was rare. People did not marry for love or with the romantic notions fostered by the novels and films of today, but generally an appreciative affection deepened over the years. It was assumed that love is the natural condition among people and that it would grow between any two who set their minds to live together and make a new family. Among our people unmarried young women had a dowry. Young couples built their own summer lodges in warm weather, and in winter lived in a longhouse with the woman's family. Our people were mostly monogamous, but sachems and medicine people or elders of great influence, who perhaps needed a larger household to carry the burdens of increased hospitality and ceremony, often had multiple spouses. In such households the first wife was usually the head of the lodge and had to approve of any subsequent wives, often selecting them.

Women dressed skins, made clothing, wove mats for and built the summer lodges, planted, harvested and cooked the corn, beans and squash, gathered berries, medicines and shellfish, made baskets, pots and wampum. Men built long-houses, dugout canoes, made snowshoes, bowls, spoons, knives, hatchets, traps, weapons, hunted, fished, and pro-tected the family and village. Both men and women broke up fields and maple sugared together. Sometimes men helped plant and harvest, as did the children.

Traditionally, marriage for our people was a true partner-ship of equality and respect. The more a man did for his wife, the more highly he was esteemed, particularly among the women.

Children were and are considered very precious, the greatest assets of parent and nation. Since women had such a high status in our tribes, girl babies were highly valued.

A woman might have many talents and occupations: botanist, herbalist, healer, potter, weaver, tanner, artist, craftswoman, diviner — but these were always in addition to her control of the food and the lodge and the raising of children. Neither men nor women earned a living by arts, crafts, teaching, politics, religion, or even healing. Those trades were all extra, after survival work was complete, done for the enjoyment or for the calling of the talent.

The people generally had very good health, and we are told that childbirth was easier for native women than for European women. As midwives and medicine women knew herbal methods of increasing or decreasing fertility, they also understood prenatal care and were highly skilled in birthing techniques.

Babies were nursed until they weaned themselves, a matter of two or three years. They were carried close to the warmth of the body during waking hours, at first by the mother, later by grandparents, aunts, older sisters and cousins. After a few weeks they were placed nearby where they could watch the mother's activities. In the early years girls and boys played together, but soon the boys would become interested in their fathers' activities, and the girls would begin to imitate their mothers and aunts. Girls would build small play lodges, prepare food, and make clothes and baskets for their dolls.

Education was by what they saw, and since all the family slept in one room, and since sex was not a secret or shameful thing, sex education came in the same way. When a young girl first came into her moon and became a woman, she secluded herself in a "little house" or moon lodge. During that time an elder woman would come and instruct her in the responsibilities of adulthood and womanhood. She would be told that this time of the month was natural, not an occasion for fear for either man or woman. She was also taught she was then the focus of such cosmic energies that she should not come near the ceremonies or ceremonial objects of the men, as her energies might disturb theirs. A woman was taught that during this moon–time, her energies were powerfully attuned, not only to the moon, but to the earth, the fire, the winds, the sea and all waters. She could learn to use those energies at that time to connect with deep, inner, female wisdom and power, and to use that power for healing.

After the four days of seclusion, there would be a ceremony and celebration by the whole village, with feasting, singing and dancing all night. It was a merry festival, full of joking, and often an acting out of sexual desires and fantasies on the part of the older and more experienced, in a general atmosphere of tolerance and good humor. This was the most important time in a woman's life, next to the birth of her children, a powerful and magical time for all the women of the tribe.

Later, if she chose, a young woman might seek a vision and a spirit guardian by fasting for many days alone in an isolated place. Then would usually come marriage. Since there was not any wealth among our people and little sense of rank, arranged marriages were not so prevalent as elsewhere, and young people often as not made their own choices.

The day before a girl's first marriage was a busy one. In one ancient custom, she would first be buried in the ground to her neck for a time, to draw health and fertility from Mother Earth. Then she would spend much time in making little cakes for the wedding party. If she had time she might join the other young women in running races or playing doubleball or stickball. Finally she would get a massage from an experienced woman which would give physical and spiritual encouragement to her fertility. The wedding party of feasting, singing, and dancing would go on all night, and at dawn the couple would, in many areas, stand on some promontory with hands joined and face the sunrise of a new life together.

A woman was born in the company of women, grew up

in the company of girls, kept house and worked in the fields with other women.

Her social and ceremonial life was comprised of women's societies and women's clan circles. Only a very small portion of her total life was spent in the company of the opposite gender.

Since children in their earliest years were raised mainly by women, and since women were in control of the household, the moral and emotional environment of the village was very largely determined by women. The homes in which the children grew were run smoothly, without conflict or pressure. Children were treated with great affection and given good attention by grandparents and older sisters. The women worked together cheerfully, and the children were allowed to do pretty much as they pleased. The pace was slow, and there was a lot of joking and gossip. Without a schedule or a clock the work was unhurried, relaxed, and completed with care and devotion. Patience, cooperation and good humor comprised the tone of a traditional home. These, and endurance, are the qualities our women taught and continue to teach the children by their living example.

A nother important example set by the native woman was that of hospitality and generosity. Whenever anyone came to visit, all work would stop for greetings, and the visitor would immediately be fed. As long as the person stayed nothing would be withheld. The last morsel of food would be shared, and the family would go out for more. If no more food were to be had, they would apologize and feel ashamed. A visitor had to be careful about admiring something belonging to the host family for he might be given it on the spot. This atmosphere of generosity and solicitude for the guest's comfort prevails today in the homes of traditional native families.

Europeans writing of their early contact with Indian women report, again and again, that they had less hardship in their daily life than the European women they knew and yet appeared hardier and of a gentler and happier disposition. Often they also noted a sense of power and independence in the native women.

T he history of the world shows most civilizations to have developed an oppressive imbalance in the favor of men. Nowhere have there ever been found civilizations with an oppressive imbalance of power in the favor of women. It may be that women, creating homes, bearing and raising

139

children, find no need for excessive displays of power over others. Only men (and women conditioned by the dominance of men) seem to feel so insecure. But where a balance of power between the sexes is achieved, with a spiritual sense of rightness and harmony, there is security and power for all. At their best, many American Indian societies achieved that balance.

Our people, the Wampanoag, were taught their tribal ways, it is said, by Ahtookis, the wolf. That is why the wolf is the totem for our whole nation. At the center of the wolf tribe is the family, getting its power from the balance and cooperation of the male and female. The she–wolf is strong and independent. Her mate works and runs with her as an equal partner. If anything should happen to her, he will hunt for, care for, and nurture their cubs.

T he basic unity, the heart and the strength of every tribe that human beings have ever created is the family. It may be comprised or defined in various ways, but a family of some kind, a permanent group based upon blood relationship and the care of children, is the essence and soul of human society. It is through the family that human beings learn what it means to be human. A society is strong and healthy just to the extent that it supports and encourages its families.

The simplest family unit is a mother and child, but given the long years it takes to raise a human child to maturity, this unit is precarious. It is difficult for a mother to feed, clothe, house and protect herself and a child for a long period of time, and it gets harder with more children. So human males have had to learn to nurture, to care for human females and their offspring. The nurturing male is an essential part of every family. A society is strong and healthy just to the extent it teaches and reinforces nurturing and cooperation in its men, as well as in its women.

H ow does our society fare today in America? One out of every two new marriages dissolves. Men are disappearing from the family — walking away, hiding out away from home in clubs, sports, or at work, or watching the television. Children are running away from home or just disappearing into their own worlds. Older people hide from the uncaring young in retirement communities, or their children put them in nursing homes. The generation gaps widen. Never before in human history has the continuity of the generations been so broken. Never before has there been such prevalence of wife abuse, child abuse and neglect as that which continues to grow in this country today.

But if society is blighted there are also signs of health and hope. There are as many forces of liberation actively engaged as there are forces of oppression. All liberation movements are allied to one another in a common effort to make humanity more human, but I believe the most important single force to emerge in the past century is the women's movement. I say this because men, locked into roles of dominance and competition, have needed the women's force and example to break those locks and re-learn how to nurture and how to cooperate.

When men and women begin again to cooperate with and nurture each other, they will be creating the future, for it is the children who will benefit.

I am proud to say that our traditional Indian people know this strength and model it for all. The family is still central in native society. The elders are honored, the women have power and respect, and the children are treated by all with affection, tolerance, and good humor. I have felt the power of women leaders in our clans and tribal organizations. I have seen the influence of Women of All Red Nations, W.A.R.N.

The issue of family is central to all races and nationalities. We must attend to our children. We must recognize that the family, in some form, is essential to society as the place where children learn what it is to be human. It is where they learn not only how to survive, but also the reasons for survival.

I f we are to strengthen the family and community, we need to assure ourselves that both provide for the needs of its members, the needs of women, the needs of men, and the needs of children and elders. Perhaps none of the forms of community yet devised have been perfect. We can look at the best ones of the past and see why they were good, and if we want to make ours better, at least we have some solid starting places.

A strong tribe will reward a woman by making her feel powerful and secure, by recognizing her creativity and her wisdom, and by cooperatively assuming many of the burdens of survival and the care of her children.

A strong tribe will reward a man for being nurturing, for being sensitive to others, for cooperating. Since men do not give birth, they have a need to nurture as well, to be creative in other ways, to achieve and be appreciated for their achievements. We need to re-value our society so that gaining wealth and power-over and winning victories no longer confer status, so that our men are honored for their kindness and gentleness, their good humor and their generosity.

We have to trust ourselves. We have to believe that Creation knows what it is doing. Creation developed sexual difference for greater strength, and gave to the female the strength and innate knowledge to bear and raise the young and shape the future of the species. Creation developed the thinking and feeling of human beings so that we can know what is best for us. To strengthen family and community we have to open ourselves to others and communicate our needs, our fears, our desires, and our dreams. Men need to talk with each other in men's clans and societies, and women with other women in their clans and societies. Children need their own councils. And all should share their feelings with each other in councils of women, men and children together.

One important issue is the community's attitude toward marriage and sexual relations. Sexual tension often arises from the biological fact that woman's sexuality is attuned to her cycles of fertility and cleansing, whereas a man does not have the same influences or cycles. For instance, when a woman is pregnant or nursing she may lose the desire for sexual expression (although it could also increase). The community needs to consider whether a man must be bound by a particular woman's cycle, or whether he will be allowed a different expression. Over the world, societies have had many kinds of responses to this question. Whatever answers our communities develop, they need to consider foremost what will make the most stable family, with the greatest fulfillment for all its members.

If our communities are balanced with men and women who feel secure and powerful, they will reinforce each other. If our women appreciate the nurturing, the cooperation, the potential for learning and sensitivity of our men, and if our men appreciate the wisdom and the strength, the intelligence and imagination and creativity of our women, together we will create the families, the tribes, and the nations that will sustain and nourish all of us and help our children manifest the divinity that lies within them.

In the distortions of male domination and aggression, many women today have become lost and confused. Many turn away from motherhood and familyhood under a system that oppresses mothers and families. Many have abortions, or abandon or abuse their children. And yet the voice of

Creation still sings in the soul of woman, stirring ancient memories deep within her. When women, however hurt or angry, find each other, touch that nurturance in each other, they begin to heal and grow strong. Nurturing each other they learn again trust and love. Feeling the power of that strength and love, men grow ashamed of their aggression and dominance and seek to learn to nurture and cooperate.

The Shawnee spoke of the Creation Spirit as "Our Grandmother." They would pray that Our Grandmother would tell the winds to heed the calls of the women people, and the women would promise that they would always listen for the songs of Our Grandmother on the winds.

Yes, the Song of Creation is there in the heart of our Sacred Mother, the Earth, and in the blood of every woman. To create peace on earth, heal the planet, cease all wars and aggression, crime and oppression, to fashion a society which is nurturing, cooperative, loving and good-humored, what is needed is for the women of the world to take control of the home again and teach the next male generation. Women in touch with their womanspirit, with the earth and each other, can make their full power felt in the villages and in the nations again.

The family, the tribe, the continuation of the species, all depend on the renewing cycles of the Mother Spirit, the pulse of the living earth that stirs the ancient wisdom of our women people — the daughters of Creation.

Chapter Twelve

Sons of Earth and Sky

"Grandfather, where did I come from?"

That was a favorite question when I was a boy.

"You are a child of earth and sky," my grandfather would say, taking me on his lap. I would lay my head against him and quietly wait for the familiar story to come.

"Of course, you come from your mother and your father, and they came from their mothers and fathers, and so on back to First Woman and First Man, and they were made of earth and sky. Before there was earth and sky, there were the stars. And the stars were far and scattered and lonely, so Creator told the starmakers to make some families for them.

"For Grandfather Sun, Hobomoko made two sisters. They were Grandmother Moon and Grandmother Ocean, and they loved each other very much. When Grandfather Sun saw Grandmother Moon, how serene and peaceful she was, he wanted her to be his wife. Then he looked down at Grandmother Ocean and saw how lively and playful she was, and how she shone under his gaze, and he loved her too. He did not know what to do. He asked the sisters if one of them would like to have him for a husband. They said that they did not want to part from each other, and that they each would like him for a husband.

"That solved the problem for Grandfather Sun, because he did not want to leave either one.

"And so they all came to make one family. Grandmother

Moon and Grandfather Sun did not have any children to-
gether. They were more like brother and sister. But Grand-
mother Ocean and Grandfather Sun had many children,
including the sky, the winds of all directions, and the earth.
When Mother Earth was delivered out of the womb of Grand-
mother Ocean onto the back of the Great Turtle, she was
embraced by Father Sky. From this came the seed of all life.
Maushop created forms for these seeds, flowers, grass, trees,
animals, birds and fish. He fashioned bodies for the human
beings out of the colored earth and for their minds he took
some of the spirit of sky. It is good to remember where we
come from, that our bodies are at home here on this soil, that
one day they will return to our mother, the earth, but that our
minds are free to run with the winds and the stars."

Now we are on a wooded hill in Mashpee, at the ceremonial fire of the Mashpee Wampanoag. Years ago, when this
particular land had first been restored to the tribe by the
town, I came here with Slow Turtle, the medicine man for
Mashpee at that time, to select this site for the fire, to build
the ceremonial arbor, and to organize the first spiritual unity
conference of the Wampanoag Nation. Many nations from the
northeast attended that conference, and many elder men
and women came and shared their wisdom. After selecting
this site, Slow Turtle and I worked together in silence on it
for the rest of the day. In that silence and common task
there was a true companionship. The Wampanoag Nation
was just beginning to rebuild itself at that time, and eventually Slow Turtle became Supreme Medicine Man for the
whole nation. Since then, he and I have worked together on
many projects involving native people, the environment, and
world peace.

Looking around me now at the arbor and the firepit, I
think back to that day when we worked together here,
saying little, yet somehow strongly connected in a bond of
respect and friendship that men sometimes feel in a common work task. I think of how both of us have tried to
extend that circle of respect and friendship to other men,
men who are trying to deal with the hurt and isolation and
conflicts put upon them by society. One of Slow Turtle's and
my major preoccupations is providing native services in
prisons. In our prison circles we often form strong relationships with men in the worst of circumstances, some of
whom have done terrible, unspeakable things. But in every
case these things are directly attributable to the terrible, unspeakable things that were done to them as men, as human

beings. Inside the protecting macho armor of these convicts is a warm, sensitive, loving, and terribly hurt little boy who has lost hope of the world ever being safe enough for him to come out. Our circles have created just enough safety for them to realize their inborn humanity is intact under those mountains of distress, and to kindle a spark of hope that they may some day be able to reclaim all their inherent goodness and build meaningful, creative lives for themselves. Yet our society continues to treat them as another species, degraded, hopelessly depraved and evil. As I think of them I wonder if you ever think of them. Do you ever wonder what this society is doing to its good, little boys to turn them into angry, fearful, bewildered and hostile animals glaring at each other from opposite sides of iron bars?

As I lie back and look at the sky, I think of myself as a child. I knew I was a good boy, but many times the world around me either didn't care, didn't notice, or thought I was actually bad. I felt very connected to nature, to all of Creation, but alone in the world of men.

I can remember when I was a little boy, perhaps four or five years old, lying on my back on the grass, looking at the deep, endless blue of the sky. I could feel the earth cradling me, supporting me, and bearing me securely upward into that vast expanse. My body felt safe in the arms of my mother, and my mind was free to explore infinity and reach toward eternity.

I knew then that I was a living part of a living universe, and I felt deeply my grandfather's truth, that I was a child of earth and sky. The earth was my mother, my home, familiar and safe. The sky was my father, a distant mystery, an excitement, a wonder, a challenge to adventure, to learn, to grow beyond my roots, to send my thoughts like maple wings and dandelion — down upon the winds toward the sun and to the stars beyond.

I knew that I was a boy and would one day be a man. I was not told, when I was very young, what that meant. I could only tell that my father, my uncles, my grandfather and great-grandfather were different from my mother, my aunts, my grandmothers and great-grandmothers.

When I did begin to get information about what it was to be a man, that information came through the dominant culture, and it was not reassuring. It was scary and hurtful. As a man I could not cry. I could be beaten, but I must not cry or I might be beaten even more. As a man I must not ever be afraid. As a man I must face violence with violence. I was encouraged to fight, and told that if I did not, I would be a coward and not a real man. It was implied that my genitals were ugly, shameful, and disgusting. They must not be seen or touched. Boys and men did not get physical affection. When we were very young, boys could be hugged and kissed by their mothers and grandmothers, but soon people began to call us babies when we sought our mother's arms, and so we pulled away in order to be men and cut off more of our feelings and our nurturing.

Now you understand that these were not the old ways of our people. Our traditional ways began to disappear along with our lands. My mother's family, Anglo and Swedish, had lost their tribal ways two thousand years before. It was no one's fault, and all my family was doing the best they knew how with the information they had.

We are all people caught in changing cultures, trying to make sense out of what has happened to us and what is happening to our children. Hear the story, then, of one man caught in these shifting cultures and consider in it the plight of all men today.

In school I was taught that other boys were competitors and enemies. Boys ridiculed each other, shamed and humiliated each other, attacked each other, feared each other. It seemed they always needed to find someone to ridicule. If you ridiculed others you might keep from being ridiculed. You made yourself an insider by scorning outsiders. It happened that, wherever I went (and my family moved several times), I was always an outsider and so were the few friends I had. One might have allies and friends but dared not be too close to any of them. If you were too smart in class, other boys would hate you. If you were not good in athletics they would despise you.

Girls were supposed to be delicate, clean and dainty, while boys were supposed to be rugged, foul and brutal. Then when we grew up we were supposed to protect and provide everything for our wives and our children. The way we were taught, it looked as though we were to be drones in constant service to our queens, automatons who took care of everything without feelings. We watched our fathers grimly carrying on, distant and unapproachable, but the ultimate authority in everything. A man was supposed to be in charge and responsible, making all decisions without consultation. We could see that we were supposed to be able to handle everything ourselves and never ask for help. Whatever life brought us we were to take on the chin, "take it like a man," with a stiff upper lip.

When I was eleven I was sent to military school and I began to learn something else about being a man. Men were the ones who had to carry guns and go out and kill other men. They were the ones who became heroes by giving their lives to save the country and to protect the women and children.

I was twelve in December of 1941. I was in full dress uniform, carrying an old Springfield rifle and marching with my school up and down a hot parade ground in Florida on that memorable Sunday when the news came that the Japanese had bombed the U.S. military and naval forces at Pearl Harbor in Hawaii. I can remember Navy fighter planes roaring overhead in a clear blue sky, the palm trees waving softly above the line of observers murmuring together somberly, my mother watching us march and weeping because the country was at war, and I would soon be a man. For myself, I was eager to go and kill those inhuman beasts that everyone said were causing all this trouble.

I did not get into that war. I was drafted into the Army at the time of the Korean "police action." I can recall the precise moment, on the firing range, when I aimed my M-1 rifle at the target silhouette of a man and knew I could never pull the trigger if there were a real human being out there. I could not shoot at some unknown man with a life of his own a hundred yards away. I began to weep as I squeezed off shots while aiming ten feet above those waving targets. How did we ever get ourselves into this crazy, disgusting predicament?

By that time I had also learned that we were allowed to get affection only from a woman, and the only manly way to get that was to seduce her sexually. In fact, the more women you were successful in getting into bed, the more of a man you were. I wanted desperately to be a "man," but I was not successful in that department at all, so it was not easy for me to think well of myself. I was a failure as a man again.

At that time, before the "sexual revolution," it was fine for men to try to seduce women. They were supposed to do that, and to be successful in order to prove their manhood. But women were not supposed to let a man do that. They would get a bad reputation, would be thought "easy," "loose," and immoral. It was a crazy situation. Men had to be the ones who pursued, and I was painfully shy and unsure of myself. I kept trying to be a great lover, failing miserably, and lying a lot about it.

Finally, when I was 19, a woman came to bed with me.

The woman lay compliantly naked and passive on my college dorm cot and expected me to do everything. I tried to act very cool, but I was nearly petrified with fear and mortification. I had only an academic and hearsay understanding of what to do. Somehow I managed to fumble and blunder through my obligations and felt only relief that it was over. It was an experience, not of intimacy, but of bewildering alienation.

At 25 I got married for the first time, for all the wrong reasons: loneliness, frustration, neediness. I married to prove I was strong and reliable, and with a romantic vision of a powerful, working partnership that was not realistic considering who we were. Because of my male training to be the strong, wise, dependable provider, I tried to take care of everything and stayed in that marriage for years after everyone else could see that it was not good for either of us.

Then I was ready to emerge as a great lover, admired by all women and envied by all men, when the women's liberation movement began to broadcast the information about how women were being oppressed. It was immediately evident to me that they were right. It was all too true. Women were not given the same opportunities by society as men. And it seemed that men were the very willing agents of this suppression and subjugation. I learned how oppressive and sexist my attitudes and assumptions were. If women had not had access to power equally with men in this society, then I felt I must give up all power myself from that time on, step back from any leadership at all, and let the women take over. I did not feel that I was being patronizing. As the beneficiary of an unjust system, I felt I must now sacrifice my ill–gotten gains – and more. Since men had set this system up, I felt I must assume responsibility again, shoulder the blame, and apologize in the face of understandable feminist anti–male rage. So I felt even worse about myself.

The trouble with my stance was that it abandoned women to the isolating and alienating burdens of leadership without real support. The only place where I felt good was in my role as a father. There I could assume responsibility. I love my children, all children, and I love giving my time and attention to them. My devotion was natural to me, and right in line with women's needs, so I got approval for that.

In order to understand myself and to learn how to be a better ally for women, I began to find men's groups, where we would hear each other out and support each other. As we celebrated ourselves as men, we began to realize that we were not oppressors. We were the agents of the societal oppression of women, to be sure, but we were unwilling agents. None of us had asked for that role. We had not understood that role, and we did not want to be in that role. And we were also the victims of oppression.

Yes, we men are also oppressed. It's oppressive to be placed in an oppressor role to begin with. It keeps us from having warm human relationships with our sisters.

It is oppressive to be the ones who must go out and, in the name of our manhood, kill other men and risk being killed by them.

It is oppressive that we are prohibited, in the name of our manhood, from expressing our feelings of grief, hurt, shame, fear, and almost everything else except anger and joy. The expression of feelings is healing. Without that expression, our wounds deaden our feeling until we become rigid and numb.

It is oppressive that we are taught to be rivals and competitors, to fear other men, to be isolated from each other and to be unable to be nurtured by men. The homophobia inflicted upon us is oppressive. It is oppressive to us, as well as to women, that we may only seek women for our nurturance. It places too great a burden upon our relationships with women. It is oppressive that we are taught we can only find intimacy and affection through sexuality, so that our sexual feelings become compulsive, causing further strain on our relationships with women and further frustration.

It is oppressive that men are taught they must be the all–wise, all–knowing protectors and providers, working and worrying themselves to an early grave to "take care of the family."

I have a friend who often gives talks on men's oppression and asks the women in the audience some very instructive questions. I'll ask some now. If any of you women want to understand men and what it is like to be a man, ask yourselves what it might be like if you were in a society where women subjugated men. How would it feel to be seen as tyrants by men you wanted to be close to.

What would it be like if women, in the name of their womanhood, had to go out and kill other women?

What would it be like if from infancy you were taught it was unwomanly to weep or show your grief?

What would it be like if you could not touch or get close to other women? What would it be like if the only intimacies society approved of were sexual, if it were unwomanly to be

151

affectionate or tender?

What would it be like if you were taught that your functions were to assume all responsibility, make all decisions, never be wrong, and work to provide for all of your family's requirements, incidentally supplying occasional seeds for reproduction?

Let us consider now the old ways of the men of my people.

I hope by now you understand that not all of the original societies on this continent were alike, or that not all had achieved ideal social organizations of total harmony, justice and prosperity. But almost every native nation was more harmonious, just and egalitarian than any of the "developed" nations of today. What's more, they lived without great want or back–breaking labor. Inequality and oppression are the creatures of economic domination. Very few societies in the Americas had built social organizations based upon accumulating great wealth and placing it in the hands of headmen and priests, together with the incumbent domination of lower classes, women, children, and slaves. In most of Europe and Asia that was the norm. In the Americas, Australia, Oceania and much of Africa, it was the exception.

There is quite a bit of popular fiction these days about European tribal peoples tens of thousands of years ago. Some of these books show those clans as fiercely hierarchical and male–dominated. I don't know if that is a true picture or an assumption. I do know it was not true on this continent.

For the many millions of people living in the Americas, all but a handful developed strong tribal ways that were respectful of each individual in the society. Women and men were balanced and equal in their power and influence, children and elders were honored and heeded. Women who felt called to take up traditional men's roles and become warriors and hunters, and men who felt called to take up traditional women's roles in the lodge and village were honored as being very special. People who were courageous enough to do things that others would not do were held in great awe.

Let us speak of some of the ways of men in these elder societies. When a baby was born a man would be equally pleased whether it was a girl or a boy. In male–dominated societies female babies were not valued by the men. Only a son brought honor, because only a son could inherit the father's wealth, property and influence. But in egalitarian tribes a woman's status, honor, influence and wealth would be no less than a man's.

It was true that most roles were specific either to a man
or a woman. So boys spent more time in the company of
men, learning men's ways, as the girls spent more time with
the women. These roles were not oppressive to either sex.
They contributed to the ease and efficiency of tribal work,
but, as I said, an exceptional individual could choose the
opposite role or transcend traditional roles.

Men were of the the greatest importance in the life of a
boy. In the early years, when the boys were too small to
travel out with the fathers and older boys, it was the grandfathers who were often closest to them. Grandfather's knowledge of the ways of their people, of the stories and the lore,
of the relationship of human beings to the rest of Creation,
formed the background of a boy's understanding of what it
was to be a man of his people. As he grew older his uncles
and elders within his clan would become more important as
teachers and guides. This sense of kinship is so strong that
even today people will call all men of the next older generation "my uncle," and men of the generations before that
"grandfather," whether related by blood, clan, band, or
friendly alliances.

At some point in early adolescence a boy's elders — his
father, grandfather, clan uncles, chief, and medicine man —
will feel the boy is ready to be a man. For this time is
devised an initiation, a rite of passage.

As the ceremonial medicine man of my band, this is one
of my functions. The boy spends a certain amount of time
alone in a designated natural area. Then he is brought to
the sweat lodge, where he recounts his experiences while
alone. Then he will pray for a vision to guide him in his life.
The elder men in the lodge will appreciate the boy's
strengths, and praise him for being so serious in his determination to follow his people's traditions, and to devote his
power and his good thinking to serve his family and his
nation. They tell him how fortunate the nation is to have
such a devoted new warrior. Every boy who cares enough for
the ways of his people to follow their rites of passage will
learn and grow much and will feel himself to be a part of
something ancient, deep and wonderful.

At the next ceremonial council the initiate will be presented as a new man of the nation. At that time he may be
given a new name, indicating his power, vision, or special
kinship in the Creation. Words will be said by his elders and
others in appreciation of this fine young warrior, who will
then be expected to say a few words from his own heart.

153

This ceremony is generally concluded with a give–away. This is how we do it.

Often I have known these young men from the time they were very young. I may have watched them grow, year by year, running and laughing with the other children at the ceremonies. I will have told stories to them many, many times, and told them about the history of our people. I will have heard them, as they grow older, begin to speak in the children's council that I call each year at Sequanakeeswash ceremonies. When their fathers come and say they are ready to make that final step to manhood, I am just as proud as they are. Now I see the young man step away from the children, filled with serious intent and dedication. I see they are ready, and I feel a sense of awe. For I know that it is not I, or the father, uncles, grandfathers, or even the traditions that have transformed the carefree boy to the responsible man who stands before me. He will care about his people, about his relatives and his nation, and he will raise his children one day in this way, with love and concern, looking to the past and the future. He will not feel this a burden, for he will not be isolated, but will know the support of the entire nation. His sons will wish to be like such a man of vision, strength and caring.

Such a transformation is fashioned by no man. It comes from within, from the hand of Creator. It is a mystery and a miracle, like watching a birth.

The dominant culture has remnants of such rites in school graduations and such organizations as Boy Scouts. But these do not lead to a closer kinship and support within the community. Rather they hurl the young out into a world of competition and alienation. Now it seems that the imbalance of male domination has created feminism and the women's movement, and that in turn has given inspiration and impetus to the men's movement, where men are supporting each other and seeking a better society.

The men's movement has not been publicized as much as the women's movement, but it is widespread and growing. At first, that movement's most important and liberating direction was to support the women's movement, although there have been also some reactionary tendencies against feminism in a small but vocal minority, just as there are also a few women who inveigh against the women's movement. Being good allies for women in their struggle and raising the consciousness of other men in that regard is still a significant contribution that men's groups are making. I know of some groups who do childcare for women's demonstrations, and some who go into schools to talk to young men about the problems of rape and the abuse of women.

But now men are also beginning to educate themselves and others about their own oppression. They are beginning to break through the terrible barriers that have kept them apart from each other, isolated and alienated them, made them rivals and competitors, kept them from natural human closeness and love for each other.

At a weekend men's gathering where ninety-five men came together, we participated with trust and openness, and found we were unafraid to show deep feelings, display physical affection, play together, dream together, and support each other in our deepest spiritual aspirations.

In this movement, men are learning how they have been hurt by the hurts of their fathers. They begin to stop blaming their fathers for their mutual alienation, and often begin reaching out to their fathers to get close to them and heal those relationships. They are learning to reach out to their sons and daughters, to be more loving, supportive fathers, unafraid to show their tenderness and nurturing. The deepest feelings, the greatest love I have found in life is in my relationship with my sons. In the security of that love I have been able to reach out again to my own father. He has responded, and, after a lifetime of distance and hurt, we are now closer than we have ever been. Through these deep bonds, I share the mystery and wonder of being a man and understand better my brotherhood with all men.

At present, the most rewarding and inspiring work I am doing is in a maximum security state prison for men. Once a week we hold an evening circle, and once a month I conduct a sweat ceremony in a sweat lodge the men and I constructed together on the grounds, in the shadow of a guard tower. People on the staff of the prison have marveled at the transformations of the men in this group and tell me it is the most successful program they have ever had.

What is different about our prison group? There's no preaching, no moralizing, no psychologizing. In the circle, we burn some sage and say a prayer with tobacco to remind us of who we are and of our relationship to Creation. Then we pass the talking-stick. The only stipulation is to be real; to be honest with ourselves and each other. Anyone may speak as long as he likes about whatever is on his mind or in his heart. Everyone respects the speaker and gives good attention. I also get people to form pairs and share feelings with each other one-to-one. This way many more express themselves who are not comfortable doing so in the group. In the sweat lodge the men are encouraged to discharge painful emotions that have been suppressed, and to examine and let go of destructive thinking patterns, to reach for their highest visions, and hear the voice of Creation in their hearts.

A great change has come over the men who have been consistent and devoted in attendance over a period of time. They no longer feel a need to act tough and macho and impress the other inmates with how bad they are. They can be gentle and tender with each other. They can hug each other in public and say, "I love you, brother," and no one thinks that strange or funny. They can even show their sadness and weep openly.

At our last circle an older man introduced a young man whom he said he loved like a son, and, since the brother was in pain, he had asked him to come for the first time and speak. The young man said his mother had died, and went on to say just how that felt to him, that for the first time in his life he felt completely on his own, and it was scary. He went on to talk about what his life had been like growing up, and how no one in the prison really knew him because he felt he had to keep a hard mask between him and the world, but that really he was a soft and caring person inside. By the time he finished there were tears in everyone's eyes. Man after man stood up to speak of his feelings, how deeply he had been moved, how open he was for other brothers to come to in time of need, how much that closeness they had established meant to them.

The older men reach out to the younger inmates to keep them out of trouble and guide them towards a positive future. Every one of them has begun to think in a creative way about changing not only themselves and their lives, but the lives of those around them, and of creating a world free of the inequities and injustices that brought them to confinement in a penal institution.

The brotherhood among these men is devoted and true, and it is one of the great joys of my life to feel a part of that. I love each one, and know they love me. I look forward to going to see them with the eagerness of one going home to his family. I share in their joys and griefs and frustrations and in their determination to change and refashion their lives. They show me the meaning, the possibilities of true brotherhood and familyhood. Their struggles are hard, but they assume them gracefully, with courage, humor, and love.

This year I have begun to go a second night each week

to teach a class in peer counseling. There, a group of men dedicated to changing their lives, are conscientiously exploring their feelings and becoming clear and constructive in their thinking, learning to help each other deal with the hurts and struggles of life. I believe these men will not only be able to fit into society once more, they will know how to counsel young people becoming involved with drugs and crime, to bring people together to uproot oppression, and to become leaders in helping to transform their society into one that is more just and more humane.

Here in this refuse pit of society's blunders, men with tattooed bodies and hearts scarred by crimes of violence both by them and against them are discovering and demonstrating what it means to be human. These men have committed murder, rape, robbery, drug dealing and other violent crimes, and they look back on those actions with wonder and regret. It feels to them as though they had been in the grip of some powerful force they could not understand. Somehow they recognize that their essential goodness had been interfered with by circumstances that were not of their own making. The wisdom our traditions hold is illumined by these most distressed men who are finding, often for the first time, the love in their hearts, the clear creative thinking of their minds, and the will to dedicate their energies to a vision of a possible world of true freedom and justice.

Sometimes when I watch one of the gray–faced leaders of business or government speak, I begin to feel discouraged for the future of humanity. Then I think of my brothers supporting the elder women at Big Mountain. I think of my brothers standing security watch in the Black Hills. I think of my brothers tenderly caring for their infant children. I think of my brothers supporting our sisters' struggles for liberation. I think of my heterosexual brothers unafraid to walk side by side with my gay brothers in defense of their rights. I think of my brothers who are dedicating their lives to peace, to saving the earth, to ending hunger, torture, and political imprisonment, to saving the whales, the dolphins, the seals, the wolves, and all our other relatives. I think of my brothers gathering in small groups to support each other. I think of my faithful brothers in prison. Through this I understand more of the full glory of manhood, and I am proud to be a man.

Chapter Thirteen

The Dreams of The People

*"Come closer around the fire,
let us speak the dreams of our people..."*

*The firekeeper stirs and re-arranges the burning logs. The
flames throw taller gestures with a renewed warmth and
brightness that glows on the faces in the circle of listeners.
The fire sparkles again in each eye in the circle, from the very
young to the very old. All are quiet, intent upon the words of
the storyteller, weaving a tale of long ago, a tale of magic and
wonder, a tale of beauty and love, a tale of terror and mystery, a tale of folly and trickery. Fear, hope, sadness and
laughter tremble in the heart of every listener.*

This is a very ancient scene. Night after night from time
immemorial little groups of people have gathered in the
villages of all the races of humankind all over the planet to
share the spell created by the most ancient of arts: the
telling of tales.

Among my people this will happen whenever we gather
together, especially during the times of our ceremonies. The
storyteller may be an old woman or old man, or sometimes a
younger person remembering stories of the old ones heard in
childhood. At ceremonies too we may tell our dreams. As
individuals we have many kinds of dreams: strange, colorful,
funny, erotic, frightening. They tell us something we may not

understand about ourselves, about who we are, about the
mysterious depths of our subconscious life, about our past
and our future. Our people can understand the Dreamtime
of the Australian native people, a reality accessible in
dreams of a spirit world that is the substance of Creation of
which waking experience is the shadow. Stories are the
dreams of the people — a people full of mysteries and
marvels, humor and desire, fear and passion. They tell us
who we are, where we have come from, where we may
be going.

Stories probe our collective unconscious. They illuminate
our common visions, nightmares, and aspirations. The
stories of a people tell much about them.

Storytelling is an art kept vital among people who retain
their identity and traditions. Today, as many cultures seek
to preserve their identities, the art of storytelling is being
revived, and that is a good thing for all people.

Stories not only mirror a people, they also illuminate
their passages. As children we learn and grow by imitation.
We imitate those around us, the models of those older than
us who show by their actions what it is to be a human
being in society. And we imitate the models provided by the
stories we hear.

Stories are healing. My grandfather told me that when I
was small, but I didn't understand. I loved to listen to his
stories and always asked for more, but I couldn't have told
you why. I didn't think then that it might be because the
stories made me feel good. But they did. Good and powerful
and alive. Because I loved stories I began to tell them, and
so I was a storyteller before I understood the healing power
of that art. I learned somehow that the function of any art
is to illuminate, but I don't think I noticed how that illumi-
nation is a fundamental source of healing. I did see that
hearing stories had a powerful effect on people. Reading
Aristotle explained to me how people's feelings are stimulated watching drama and how that is cathartic and healing
for them. I also could see how healing laughter is, and
humor played a major part in my stories.

Thus storytelling led me directly into the path of healing.
It was precisely when I realized that my stories, presented
dramatically on the stage, were not healing enough that I
left the world of theater and art to seek understanding and
wisdom. I was making people laugh at their problems and
the problems of society, and that was good, but it wasn't
enough. People might feel better for an hour or two, but it
was like a pill that relieves the symptoms but never touches

the disease. It took me many years to identify that disease
and diagnose the cause. I had to return to the traditional
wisdom, wisdom embedded in the stories I had heard as a
child but hadn't understood. After I had been instructed by
native elders, after I experienced the connections made in the
ceremonies, then I saw the world's history clearly and began
to comprehend the stories.

Very simply put, the basic disease is alienation — alienation from each other, from the earth and all nature,
from the Creation — and the cause is domination, which in
turn is caused by and causes fear in an endless cycle. The
disease is spiritual and requires a spiritual cure. The cure is
connection. Connection to ourselves, first of all, so we understand, appreciate, and love who we are. Then we must connect with each other, responding to our deep need to give
love, which is even greater than our need to be loved. Finally, we connect with the earth and all Creation, with the
source and meaning of existence.

These are the connections that art can make, the healing
that art can do. Storytelling is the oldest and most powerful
of the arts. That is why for our people it is regarded as a
sacred and healing thing. Instead of separating people from
each other, as in other media, the storyteller brings people
together, makes them participate in the event, joining their
hearts and minds in a circle of magic and imagination.

Just as a culture is shaped by its legends, so our own
individual stories become the mythology which guides our
personal journeys. Our personal stories are healing. People
have an urge to tell their own stories because they seek that
healing. People not only seek out psychiatrists and counsel-
ors to hear their stories, keep journals and write autobiogra-
phies to understand their lives, but also are trying to tell
each other their stories all the time. Just listen as you pass
them in the streets, sit by them in waiting rooms and res-
taurants. I hear them wherever I go. Each one trying to tell
her story, but the other is barely listening because he can't
wait to interrupt and tell his own story.

One of my most popular workshops is one I call "Your
Life Is a Healing Story." I explain how healing it is to tell
your own story and how people are trying to do that all the
time. But their attempts aren't very effective because hardly
anyone listens. We are concerned about being heard, of
course, because we need to be heard, and we deserve to be
heard. That's why professional counseling is in such demand. If we all were to realize that, there is a simple thing

we could do: we could agree to take turns being listeners. It's as simple as that — just agree to take turns, and when it's your turn to listen, really listen without interrupting, giving advice, or inserting any of your story.

In the workshop I get everyone into groups of three so each one can have time to speak while the other two listen. Then I have each storyteller describe herself as the protagonist of her own story, describe some goal that she wanted in the past, describe the obstacle to her obtaining that goal, and tell the story of how she succeeded in obtaining it. Success stories are very inspiring and empowering. It would help us to tell them more often. I also have them tell a story about a goal they have for the future and how they will obtain that. Thus they become the author of their own lives.

In other classes I teach the art of listening, and how to arrange times with sympathetic people to tell personal stories, to listen, support and encourage each other. Simply by arranging to tell their own stories regularly to supportive listeners, thousands of people all over the world are learning now to make sense of their lives, how to take control and create their own lives with intelligence and passion.

All over the world right this minute millions of little children are learning their own languages all by themselves with all the literary gusto of a Dante, a Cervantes, a Victor Hugo, or a Thomas Mann. And they all could become wonderful storytellers too, but only a few will develop this verbal skill. I know which ones they are. They are the ones who have someone to tell them stories, and someone to listen to them and appreciate their stories. Children love stories. People of all ages love stories. Don't you love stories? Of course you do. Why is that? Maybe it's because our lives roll on from birth to death, and it's kind of hard to get a view of that whole thing when you are in the middle of it. But a story has a beginning and you know you are going to get to the end and understand the whole thing. You may be afraid or worried or horrified, but you know you are going to get to the end and see the story as a whole. How different our reactions in life would be if we could view life as a story which we could enjoy in its entirety and realize after, there might be other stories.

That's why I like being a storyteller. It touches something universal and common to all human beings. Through stories I can relate to all ages, all nationalities, all races, all classes of people equally. I love to listen and encourage the storytelling of others, especially children, who haven't forgotten yet how important stories are.

T he most powerful teachings of the world's great sages are in the form of stories and parables. The stories of Rama, Krishna, Gautama, Milarepa, Moses, David, Jesus, Mahomet have essential truth. All had great power in history. Perhaps if those stories were taught as more important and interesting than the stories of the Khans and the Caesars, the history of civilization would be different. Certainly it would be different if there were an equal or greater number of stories of great and powerful women.

Our mythology shapes our values and our dreams. Generations of people have learned of valor from Achilles, of shrewdness from Odysseus, of simplicity from Francis of Assisi, of rebellion against legal injustice from Robin Hood, of the courage to follow a vision from Joan of Arc. So too in our native nations we have models to illuminate our journeys: Maushop, Weetucks, Glooscap, Deganawida, Hiawatha, Manabozho, Sweet Medicine, Raven, Coyote and many others.

If you want to learn about a culture, look at its mythology. What are the connections the people of that culture make in their stories? What can you know of the people of Africa or Asia or Europe by the stories they tell? No doubt people change faster than their stories. Some of the changes are good, and some are not so good. So we may look to traditional stories to find lost wisdom from the past, and we can also see places where we may have begun to outgrow the ignorance, superstition and bigotry of earlier times.

Technology and the way it is used has profoundly affected culture. In primitive societies all the arts are accessible and the creativity of all people is encouraged. Each one expresses individual as well as group consciousness in creating stories, songs, artifacts, paintings and carvings. As technology advances, art becomes more and more the province of professionals. On the positive side this has encouraged individual artists, in Europe, for example, who have risen to the glorious heights of Michelangelo, Shakespeare, and Bach. On the other hand it has helped to diminish the ordinary person's sense of individual creativity. With technology comes expense, and the control of art shifts into the hands of entrepreneurs, governmental or private, who build and own the publishing houses, television stations, recording companies, museums, galleries, theatres, and all the advertising and distribution of art to the public.

We can see this process in operation today. Among our people in remote areas where there is as yet little of twentieth century technology, there is a very high degree of individuality in storytelling and singing, as well as in carving and painting, and the making of clothing and baskets. But as higher technology invades, the people forget how to do these things for themselves. They rely on radios, television and magazines for their music, their stories, and their pictures of the world. Today we have many wonderful native artists, potters, painters, jewelry makers, poets, novelists, singers and musicians, but our children are not learning to do these things themselves. In my town there is a man who travels far to the north to learn from the Cree old ones the arts of making beautiful intricate snowshoes and the nearly lost craft of building birch bark canoes. The old people are happy to see and teach him when he comes, because their own young people are no longer interested in learning these things.

There are studies now that show that when mass entertainment such as television comes to a community, the creativity of the children of that community begins to disappear. More and more we are not thinkers or creators but absorbers and consumers.

The culture of the Inuit people has traditionally been based upon their dreams. In a land where winters are dark and long, much of their richness of mind is expressed in dreams. Upon waking, the people used to tell each other their dreams, and the telling was elaborate and vivid. Dreams gave them their songs and visions of the world of the spirit. In a place of harsh, barren landscapes with little color, they expressed their dreams in carvings and paintings of fantastic shapes and brilliant hues. The art of the Inuit is one of the richest in the world, probing human imagination and the spirit that stirs deep layers of feelings in our own consciousness. But all this has changed in this century. As magazines and recordings, radio and television have entered those traditional communities, the Inuit, like the rest of us, are becoming more and more consumers and imitators, and the dreams of those people are being forgotten in the blare of mass media.

If stories mirror a culture, what is revealed by the stories of the dominant culture of today? What is the mythology of American society? What are the guides given young people to show how they should walk and shape their world?

The mythology of American society in the last half of the twentieth century is to be found on television. The average American household has at least one of its several television sets on six hours every day of the year. The average. Since most of the people I know don't have a T.V. or don't watch it very often, I figure there's got to be a lot of people watching a lot more than six hours a day. Much of that viewing is being done by children.

And what are the children of today's society watching? In one half of all the shows every night in America at least one violent crime is portrayed. Children's programs are filled with gunfire, space wars, robotic mayhem, super heroes and super villains. And those are just the cartoons. Almost every hour of prime time contains at least one crime show with predictable and obligatory shoot-outs and car crashes. Fifteen minutes of every hour is spent trying to persuade people that to be a successful and content human being they will have to buy a lot of junk they don't need.

What is the allure that keeps people addicted to this medium? There are a number of factors, but the primary one is the most ancient: stories. Stories exert a magic power, even when they are not very good. Stories are the way natural tribal peoples have always educated their young. Civilization is still doing this, but the storyteller today is the television industry. The purpose of that industry is not to teach love and sharing, generosity and hospitality; the purpose of the television industry, like that of other industries, is to make money, and in the process they teach consumerism and create addictions to false needs.

By the time the children have grown to adulthood these days, they have witnessed on television hundreds of murders and thousands of crimes of violence, robbery, inhumanity and injustice, in venal, tasteless, pointless stories. When they grow up they keep seeing and hearing the same stories, only now they have expanded into the six o'clock news and the front page headlines.

Adults are similarly addicted to stories. On television, the mythology is provided by the dramatic series — soap operas, where all the negative aspects of the culture are glamorized and the human spirit is trivialized. Even the game shows are stories, allowing ordinary folks to bring home a bundle of dreams, trips to Las Vegas, sports cars, life styles of the rich and famous.

You still only learn what the industry wants you to learn. If you are an Indian whose land is even now being stolen, whose treaty is being broken, whose water is being diverted, whose resources are being sold out by colonial puppet governments, whose health is being polluted, whose babies are being born with defects due to industrial pollution and are malnourished due to infant formula practices, or if you are an Indian woman being sterilized against your will, or if you

165

are an Indian mother in Central America whose family is being shot down for opposing a tyrannical government armed by the United States — your story will not be told on television. It will not appear in the newspapers. If you send your children to school, neither they nor their classmates will learn there of the oppression that is happening to their own people.

Our children run after each other exercising their imaginations to take on the roles of the popular heroes and heroines of television, films and comics. Whatever they see, they want to become. Even though they probably won't grow up to fly through space or live in a loin cloth in the jungle, they will carry the black and white value system of violence and narrowness as their way of seeing the world. The mind assured of a solution to a dilemma within a thirty or sixty minute segment pays a price in creativity and comprehension.

The fields of fantasy and science fiction may provide areas for examining magic and possibility in our lives and dreams, but they rarely reflect more than our concerns for survival and manipulation of the physical world. Some of the space wars achieve a kind of mythic acceptance among young and old, reflecting as they do some of our yearnings for connection and power as we conjure "The Force" to be with us. Yet, such epics and all their clones seem little more than World–War–II–flying–ace fantasies set in outer space. There's no suggestion that in the future human beings may have grown in consciousness and found other ways of relating beyond domination and rebellion, that the problems of the future will no doubt be of a very different order from those of our violent past and present.

The great phenomenon of modern publishing is the field of "women's" romance fiction. There is a rigorous regulation of this product, creating very predictable escape dreams for lonely ladies to discover the perfect lover, again and again. Since one of the most serious problems of our time is the relations between men and women, here is a medium that could provide inspiration and real challenge instead of false hopes of over–simplified ever–afters. How would it be if these lovers, instead of being caught in the patterns of romantic illusion, were to be enlightened and expanded by these encounters. Happily–ever–after does not have to be an evasion if the spiritual center of happiness is described and illuminated by the work. Even the mystery genre could be raised to the level of a vision quest.

It is a curious fact that the ethnic groups most interested

in the American Indian are the German speaking peoples. Everywhere I travel in those countries, young and old want to talk to me and to learn more about Indians. On my first trip to Germany I discovered why this is so. It is because of two authors, James Fennimore Cooper, whose Leatherstocking Tales featuring sympathetic pictures of American native people became favorites in German translation and inspired the German, Karl May, author of many adventurous romances about Indians. Even though Karl May had no firsthand knowledge of American Indians, his Apache hero Winnetu (whose name and environments seem more Algonquin than Athabascan) is believed in and loved by millions of young and old alike in Europe. So many very knowledgeable and committed allies of native people have told me that their imagination and love was stirred when they were young by the writings of Cooper and May.

It is no longer only a question of my holding on to my own culture. I want my children to live in a society that is creative, that uses all *our* resources and encourages the creativity of every member. And I want to live in a society and a community that have a true consciousness of themselves. I want to live in a society that has vision. I want to see and hear the dreams of my people.

What I am talking about is bringing our minds and our dreams together. I want us to shape the living myths that not only represent but inspire our human communities. I want us to awaken our aliveness, our creativity as a people, our sense of beauty, of possibility, and of the sacred.

What seems most lacking in the cultures of today's society is a sense of the sacred. This reflects and reinforces the spiritual malaise of the times. When the Creation is no longer seen as sacred, the people are preoccupied with death. To avoid the bleak and barren prospect of life without splendor or fulfillment and death without hope or meaning, people fill their empty dreams with material things and make objects of themselves and others, hoping power and prestige will banish their nightmares of the terrifying void. People become increasingly cynical and selfish, pessimistic and desperate. When life and the universe are not sacred, society becomes at once more aggressive and more apathetic and finds its expression in violence and drugs.

What we need is to find a common dream that connects us to Creation, that discovers the sacred, the magic in every particle of matter, space, and energy, and every moment of time. We need to evoke the deep sense of connection and relationship, the pattern that illuminates our place, our identity, direction and purpose, and addresses our deep need for meaning in existence.

And this must be done in a way that speaks to us all. We need a mythology that transcends Judeo–Christian–Moslem, or Hindu–Buddhist, or Rational–Humanistic–Scientific. We need stories and dreams we can share as children of the earth, stories that bring us to a knowledge of ourselves as global beings and as participants in a vast and wondrous unfolding of Creation.

The new renaissance of storytelling today provides a hope for us all. If you want to make a film, or a television show, or publish a book or a magazine, it will cost a lot of money. More than you have. So you will have to go to the people who have money, banks and investment firms, and ask them to invest in your idea. Naturally they are going to ask you what your idea is, and if it's not in their interest, you won't get the money. So you won't see very many alternative visions being promoted in these media. But it doesn't cost you a penny to stand up in front of an audience and tell a story. All the characters and scenery and special effects are created from your mind playing on the minds of your listeners.

We can create our own myths. We can have a vision of a world we desire and create its mythology.

A s in all of our learning, however, it is wise to look to the past for guidance. To look to the traditions that have lasted among people who have savored the wisdom of living according to Creation's ways for countless generations.

At one time, they say, there were no stories. It was a young boy, an orphan, sent hunting by his foster mother, who came upon a strange stone in the woods which spoke to him. At the stone's request the boy brought his whole village to hear the stone tell stories of the times before this world. When the stone had finished, it told the people that some of them would remember these stories and tell them to others. These would be the storytellers, and the people should give them honor and feed them wherever they might go. Each new generation must have those who would hear and remember and become storytellers, for from then on the stone would be silent and the people would have to keep their own stories.

Before I learned the sacred wisdom of our old ones, I made stories and told stories that were a mirror of the society I saw around me. Mostly my stories laughed at that society and its follies. But as I began to see how dangerous those follies were to the future of the human race, to the life of my family and friends, it grew harder to laugh. It was at that point that I stopped and turned back and went on the search that led me to the sacred path and made the Creation whole again in my mind and heart. Now for me storytelling is a sacred and healing art.

We are the keepers of the lore of our people. All of us. Those who write and tell stories have a responsibility, because of the great power of stories, to consider the healing aspect of them. And those who listen have a responsibility to demand that stories be healing, that they represent our brightest vision, and that they connect us to our inner nature, to our essential humanness. We need stories that illuminate, stories that provoke, with laughter and with tears, our deep need to love, to be playful and creative; stories of courage in the face of dehumanizing fear; stories of connection between parent and child, man and woman, woman and woman, man and man, old and young, connection between cultures and races and religions; stories that bind us in affection and pleasure and extol our common humanity; stories that connect us to life, to earth and all beings, to the blazing heavens and the vastness of empty space.

The stories you tell your lovers and friends can heal, can illuminate your relationship. The stories you tell your children can make them strong, make them feel good about themselves and about each other, can make your whole family strong. If our stories are about peace and justice, then that is what we are creating. If our stories are about alienation and fear, then that is what we are creating.

We need to give this information to the storytellers, and to the teachers of storytelling, to the departments of literature, to the prize award committees, to the publishing, television and film industries. We need to ask the famous stars who are the models for our children, are the images they portray healing or alienating? What kind of a male image is a half–naked, crazed berserker with sweating muscles, bulging jugulars, and a machine gun blazing from his hip? What kind of a female image is a helpless, seductive, glamorous plaything who needs to be rescued by a man?

As we speak here today, one of the greatest problems on everyone's mind is that of alcohol and drug abuse. It is a problem of epidemic proportions in the western world. It is destroying children, adults, and families. Everyone is concerned. We know the heart of the problem is in the demand for the drugs, which has to do with many things: economic oppression, alienation, lack of congruence, hope, love and creativity. How are these things being addressed by our storytellers? Here is an issue worth all our attention and thought. Artists, writers, producers, storytellers, need to come together and discuss the social needs and responsibilities of their professions.

We are programming our whole society with the models we are presenting to ourselves in motion pictures, television, books, magazines, and recordings. The protagonists of our stories are concerned with mere survival, or with the garnering of wealth, power or fame. The sense of victory at the end of these stories is vicarious and hollow. There is no satisfaction in life in the accumulation of these things. Beyond the life that is saved, beyond the marriage promised at the story's end remains the question: if life's meaning and joy is felt only in moments of victory, what are we to do with the rest of our lives, the "daily grind," human relationship moment–by–moment, building, creating, learning, healing?

We have accepted the premise that the world we have made isolates us from each other. Our images of contemporary life are ones of profound alienation. The images we create have much power. They have an energy of their own that stirs our feelings and shapes our perceptions of reality.

T he stories of my people I heard from my grandfather. I tell them to my sons now, and to the other children of our nation at our ceremonies. Some of them will remember these, and tell them, and so they will pass to the unborn generations. The stories speak of the Creation, of how things came to be, of how our people arose from the sea to live on islands, and how they traveled through the world, through world after world, to come to the shores where we have lived for thousands of years. They tell of the sacredness of these lands and the great strength of our people. They give our children a feeling of what it means to be given a life to live on this planet, in this universe. They give all of us a feeling of pride in the special experience and the survival of our nation. They make us feel good to be alive, to be who we are, and to share this ancient heritage.

These stories are not written down anywhere. Perhaps it is better so. I feel the life in my grandfather's stories with far greater power than that I feel in written form, including the great scriptures of the world. But I am glad to have learned other stories too, ones that were written, and that otherwise

I would not have heard. Many stories of other people which I
have read have been important to me. So maybe some day I
shall write all the stories that I only refer to as we talk here.
I will think about it, and ask for counsel from my people
and from the Great Spirit of the World. Perhaps there are so
many people who are disillusioned by the destructiveness of
modern civilization that it is time for them to know and heed
the wisdom and healing of the stories of our old ones. It is
because of that I now travel and put these teachings into
print and recordings.

I belong to a growing group of wonderful storytellers here
in New England. Through storytelling events and other gatherings that feature folk arts, we are coming to know and
delight in each others' own special material and skills. This
is a broad movement, with many regions discovering and
developing their own folklore traditions. There is a national
storytellers convention every year in Tennessee. More and
more storytellers are coming into demand for festivals, con-
certs, parties, weddings, schools, camps and hospitals, and
the revival art is becoming once more a respected and re-
warded profession. I have organized storytelling conferences
at our place in New Hampshire. My motives for doing this
are to share the concerns and joys of our profession, to
promote and extend the art, and to examine the social
values and effects of the stories we tell.

Many of the storytellers specialize in ethnic folklore —
Irish, Jewish, Russian, Scottish, Yankee. Others write their
own material or collect it from a wide range of sources. Of
course, most of my stories are Wampanoag stories, but I
have learned stories of many other Indian nations on my
travels, and I also have learned to tell stories of other cultures. A story is a treasure, wherever you find it. And so I
know some traditional Chinese, Japanese, Polynesian, Afri-
can, Jewish, Irish, Welsh, Breton, and even a few modern
stories.

Many of us are looking into the content of our stories,
both traditional and modern. Storytellers are becoming more
and more conscious of the message implied in the stories
they tell. They are looking more closely at the social implica-
tions of stories about kings and people seeking dominion
over lands and wealth, and especially of women as goals and
objects with little power or control over their own lives.

I am interested in creating a new mythology for the
children of the world. I wish all peoples to hold to the best
of their traditional culture. But I seek to go beyond that. We
live in a very new world, a world that already shares a

culture we have not created. In Germany I turn on the television and I see mostly American crime dramas and movies.

In this world, multinational corporations hold the fate of whole countries in their hands, and a small nuclear power could wipe out all cultures here forever.

In our community we have a business we call *Story Stone*. We produce cassette recordings of positive storytelling for all ages. I have recorded several cassettes of the stories of my people and the native people of Turtle Island, and we have recorded some of the best storytellers of our region and of other places. These are stories to delight and entertain, but they also create new images for us. These images arise out of a different vision of the world, a world of new possibility. They envision a different power from the power of gold and gunpowder. They are images of spiritual power, a mythology of love and of responsibility for the earth and all of life. It is a mythology of empowerment of women, of children, of elders, of all oppressed people; a mythology of the equality of all beings, of abundance and sharing, of justice and freedom from domination. It is a mythology of the possibilities of unlimited consciousness, of each person possessing their birthright of health and joy and love.

Children always ask me if the stories are true. I always answer yes. The stories are true.

All stories reflect some truth about the universe. Are some "more true" than others? Perhaps, perhaps not. But some are certainly more important than others. A trivial fact is true. Some stories, however, contain very profound wisdom that can change lives, change society and history.

All art is about truth. Music and visual arts touch deep non–verbal places of truth in the human heart. In this civilization most art and most artists are under–valued and little appreciated or supported, while a few are ridiculously overpaid. A rational society would value highly all contributions to the perception of truth and the creation of beauty and would provide encouragement and support for all its artists. The elevations of fame and wealth are irrelevant and a distraction to any true artist, but the work is honest work and a benefit to the community and should be given that recognition. A rational society would also understand that all people are innately creative and when encouraged may make delightful contributions to the beauty and stimulation of the environment. Art is the expression of Creation's yearning for awareness, for beauty and variety and order. That also is part of the new mythology we need to hear and communicate — the sublime vocation of humankind towards the beauty, harmony, and survival of life and its environment.

As a storyteller, I want to speak to all storytellers. As an artist, I seek to join with other artists to find the dreams that are buried in the depths of our souls. From all these will come our collective vision. Can any doubt that if all our art reflected the highest in human vision we would be living in a very different world today?

Storytelling has been a primary resource for the cohesion and continuity of our tribal communities, probably since the first people made fire and sat around it to share their dreams. Some people, such as the Iroquois, traditionally only told their stories during the long winter nights. Others told stories mostly during rituals at the ceremonies. My own people love stories, are inveterate storytellers, and tell them any time of day, any time of year. Perhaps that is why, despite the loss of our land and many traditional ways, our identity and culture are still strong. Storytelling has been a way of survival for us.

The lesson is this: if you want to survive as a people, if you want to retain a continuity of the wisdom of the past, then gather your families, gather your friends and loved ones, and bind them together in the magic of storytelling. Focus on the most inspiring elements of your history and establish your community mythology. Exalt the wonders of human love and compassion, shrewdness and humor. Let us laugh and weep with our children at the follies of the past and be elated and illuminated with them by the great moments of splendor and nobility. For those who create new communities, new tribes, a new tradition of stories must be created. Perhaps as we tell and spread these stories we will begin to affect the consciousness of the artists and producers who create the images in the great media industries around the planet. In any case, we will be taking responsibility for our images and visions and following the paths that we have made and chosen for ourselves.

Our art, the images we form, the stories we tell, have a great power. It shapes our dreams. By what dreams shall art be shaped? Our images and myths are conductors of psychic energy. They are able to limit or to liberate the vision of a people and its sense of possibility. Expression is part of our health and survival as individuals. Our communities need art as inspiration and expression of their identity, and the human race needs art for its survival as well. We need art that connects us, that creates bonds, establishes relationship, and illuminates the collective unconscious. Above all we need art that speaks to our deepest needs for meaning and hope, that celebrates the sacred in all Creation and in ourselves.

If we want to build community, the place to begin is with its culture. We must gather the art of the people in a place where they may see the reflection of their own dreams, a place to display their visions in fine arts, in music, dance, storytelling and theater. If you bring the people of an area together once a week to dance, to sing, to hear stories, and to listen to each other, you will have begun to create a community.

I have a friend by the name of Louie who calls himself a professor of rapology. In one of his raps he talks of the dreams of the people. He says in his neighborhood in Brooklyn you need a dream to survive, and everyone has a different dream. One dreams of being a rock star, another of winning the lottery, another of marriage and moving to the country. He says he has a dream too, because he also needs a dream to survive. His dream is that some morning, just before dawn, everyone in his neighborhood will have the same dream at the same time. Then they will make their common dream come true.

Truly, stories are the dreams of the people. We must create new stories out of our highest vision and encourage our children to dream new dreams and build their world upon them.

The firekeeper puts more wood into the flames, and the storyteller lets the images of his last tale glow like the embers in every listener's mind. He waits, watching the flames.

"Tell us another story," a child says.

"First, I want to hear you sing. We need to move our feet and dance too. Let's have the Friendship Song."

In the dancing light and shadow of the fire, the people stand and, putting a hand on the shoulder of the one ahead, they move to the shaking of rattles, spiraling in and out, singing the Wampanoag Friendship Song.

When the dance is done, the people sit again, a little closer, a little warmer, and the storyteller begins another tale.

Teller of Tales
I am anonymous
I am not to be named
I am but a Teller of Tales
A Keeper of the Mysteries and the Lore
The Wisdom and the Teachings of the Old Ones
Minatou of the Ways of the People
Come closer around the fire
And I will speak my story

I am anonymous
I am not to be named
A Singer, a Dreamer, a Seer, a Sham
Lover, Father, Brother, Child
My story began when the Fire was made
I crossed the Great Flood with our Nation
Carrying the council of the Wolf
Carrying the secrets of the Owl

I am anonymous
I am not to be named
I am the Traveler and the Path
I am the Puma and her Prey
I am the Maggot that waits for the Vulture
I am the breathing of the Stars
I am Dung, I am Ash, I am Dust, I am Lime
I am the headless Bird of Time

Say I am Movement, Ecstasy
Dear Listener, Stranger, my voice is yours
Listen to your soul for we are one
We are anonymous
We are not to be named
Come closer around the fire
Let us speak the Dreams of our People
Tell the Tales of Love and Longing
And sing the Songs of the Yet Unborn

Epilogue

We have met in council in these circles for some time, and now it is autumn again.

In Pokonoket Wampanoag country the woods and hills are aflame in blazing colors, the brilliant glowing orange of the maples, the fiery red of the oaks and sumacs, the dancing yellow of birch and ash. It is time for me to finish cutting and stacking my firewood. The autumn winds have already stripped my birch grove bare of leaves, and the branches wave and reach their naked fingers into the bluest sky of the year. A languid warmth has briefly returned to the land, the phenomenon that the English settlers marveled at and named Indian Summer.

I have tried to share with you some of the wisdom that has been transmitted in the traditions of our people. As I was taught, this knowledge is not for us alone, but is the essential teaching necessary for all human beings to live in a good way according to the laws of nature, the Original Instructions of the Creation on this earth.

I hope that it may give you something to think upon. I hope you may consider how to use this knowledge in your own life.

It is time for us to go beyond where we have been.

It is time for us to transform ourselves, transform our relationships, transform our communities, and transform society and all its institutions. It is time for us to go beyond power *over* and power *against*, and discover power *with* each other and all Creation. We must understand that power over, or domination, is a disease that contaminates whatever it touches. It creates, favors and enhances the exploiters, the oppressors, and the greedy. It installs itself in systems and institutions that, like Procrustes, mutilate and shape human nature to their patterns.

It is time for us to influence evolution in a creative and rational way. Evolution involves choice. We are always choosing. Even when you do nothing, that is a choice. When our choices are free, free from constraint by domination and the contamination of power systems, they will always be rational and creative.

It is time for us to go beyond.

It is time for us to go beyond guilt and blame. They are

177

not helpful. They are not healing. We are all in this together, and we must cherish each other and cherish ourselves.

It is time for us to go beyond our individual perspectives. It is time to remove the shackles of our personal histories, to be free and create ourselves anew.

It is time to go beyond our historical and cultural perspectives. Who you are is important. It is important to feel good about your age, your gender, your history, your culture, but we are also more than these, and we must also go beyond them all.

It is time to go beyond the human perspective. We are living beings, children of Mother Earth, relatives to all creatures.

It is time to go beyond the earthly perspective, beyond the perspective of this place and this time. We are part of something so vast it seems infinite and eternal from where we are. We cannot really know the extent of it, or understand the meaning of it, but we are certainly part of it. We are sacred beings in a sacred universe where all is in relationship. It is time to trust and cherish that relationship and tear down all our walls.

It is time to find our communality as human beings, to unify our vision and make connections. It is time to liberate ourselves and each other. We must understand human nature, our essential selves. We must distinguish people from systems and institutions, and see how these systems distort human nature.

Of all the creatures on this planet, we are the ones who create — the agents of change. It is time to integrate human creativity and our use of the tools we create, with our deepest nature, our sense of what is primal and sacred.

I hope that some of you may be thinking about how to find the path back to Creation in your lives. Perhaps you may be considering your Original Instructions, and how to live within the Sacred Circle, and how to bring that circle to your own family, to your community, to your work and to your outreach into the great world. I'm sure that if you discuss the possibility of a society of love with friends and people you meet, you will find many that understand and want that too.

So I hope that many of you will speak of these things with your families and friends and others in your community. You may wish to form a circle and meet regularly to put your minds together and consider how to transform your communities, nations, and all society. You might start a class or discussion group in your local school, church, or social organization.

You might use the councils recorded in this book as a starting point for your discussions. It is good to begin such councils by holding hands and reminding ourselves of our relationships to each other, to the earth, common mother of us all, to all the other children of the earth, our relatives of all the myriad species, and our distant unknown relatives throughout Creation, appreciating and thanking them all for their part in this great mystery of existence, and giving thanks to the Mystery itself, the Cause that brought us here, Creator. Perhaps someone might read one of the council chapters before each meeting. Then you might pass a talking stick to share the thoughts and feelings stimulated by them. There are only two instructions to the talking stick: be honest, and give respectful attention to whomever holds the stick, without comment or interruption.

I suggest that you do more than just discuss community and world situations. It is good to share personal feelings and tell your stories to each other. It is good to share our hopes and dreams, our fears and frustrations, to appreciate and support each other in manifesting our visions together. This will give your circle heart.

It is also good to take on practical projects and work together to achieve something concrete, however small. Remember, together there is nothing we cannot do. It is good to share food, singing, and dancing, to keep your times together joyful.

If you are unsure of your ability to create a circle which could support you, read Chapter Seven again. Then just jump in and do it. And let me know how you are making out.

There are many such circles meeting together around the planet at this time. It would be good to learn of each other. The circles I have helped to initiate in my travels stay connected through a newsletter, *The Talking Stick.* If you wish to connect with those circles and to let them know of your circle, write to us here at: Mettanokit Outreach
Route 123
Greenville, N.H. 03048
U.S.A.

These councils are only a beginning. There is so much more to be said. A lot is going on in the world now that very few people know about. To young people in schools and people who come to me searching, I give information about real alternatives that the system doesn't teach them about. I tell them how people are quietly making changes in their worlds, developing human cultures hidden inside inhuman societies.

Many people are looking toward indigenous earth peoples for understanding of how to live in harmony and walk in a sacred manner, and native people are looking to their elders and traditions to find this knowledge. We cannot expect to recreate the conditions of ages that have past, and few would wish to. Yet the spiritual understandings of these old ways are sound, and the spiritual foundations of modern civilization are fundamentally weak and destructive. So the question is, how can we use this knowledge, which is universal and for all-time, in the civilization we have inherited? In other words, how can we transform society today so that we may obey the Original Instructions and return to Creation?

Such a humane and harmonious society would perforce require the protection and preservation of all peoples, and especially those who are the guardians of this sacred knowledge. Therefore we also must make people aware that there are 200 million native indigenous peoples around the world who remain unknown and neglected under the domination of colonial powers on every continent. The human rights and the very survival of all these elder nations of the world are dependent upon securing their sovereignty and the protection of that sovereignty under law, which has not been anywhere established, neither in the United Nations nor among the existing governments that subscribe to that organization.

I invite you to share some more councils with me in which we will speak of these matters. These councils will be recorded and bound into another volume which will consider the conscious creation of community.

We will look into what may be done at this time to put the basic principles of this wisdom into effect in the world of today and tomorrow.

We will look at some of the ways conscious creation of community has happened in the past and is happening in many places right now, among both native and non-native populations.

We will also have four councils to speak of the four directions in a medicine wheel of community, to speak of the body, mind, heart, and spirit of community.

We will look in more detail at the experiences of our Mettanokit Community and how it functions. We will consider how other such communities could be created.

And finally we will weave a vision of a joyous and possible future for human beings upon this beautiful earth.

I invite you to communicate with me and share your experiences, questions, problems in creating and transforming your life and your community. I am glad to travel where I am invited, to meet and form circles with people, to give whatever inspiration, support, encouragement and insight I can to all who are trying to make a difference, to heal relationships, society, and the environment.

To heal, to change, to be free, to act upon your vision, these all require courage. In a society of domination and fear it takes courage to be different, to emerge, to change and create change. In a world where there is so little love, so much alienation and isolation and hostility, it takes great courage even to love.

I wish you courage.

I love you.

A PRAYER TO HUMANKIND

Hear, O Humankind, the prayer of my heart.

For are we not one, have we not one desire,
to heal our Mother Earth and bind her wounds?
And still to be free as the spotted Eagle climbing
the laughing breath of our Father Sky,
to hear again from dark forests and flashing rivers
the varied ever-changing Song of Creation.

O Humankind, are we not all brothers and sisters,
are we not the grandchildren of the Great Mystery?
Do we not all want to love and be loved, to work
and to play, to sing and dance together?
But we live with fear. Fear that is hate, fear
that is mistrust, envy, greed, vanity, fear that is
ambition, competition, aggression, fear that is
loneliness, anger, bitterness, cruelty . . . and yet,
fear is only twisted love, love turned back on itself,
love that was denied, love that was rejected . . .
and love . . .
          Love is life — creation, seed and leaf
and blossom and fruit and seed, love is growth
and search and reach and touch and dance,
love is nurture and succor and feed and pleasure,
love is pleasuring ourselves pleasuring each other,
love is life believing in itself.
          And life . . .
Life is the Sacred Mystery singing to itself, dancing
to its drum, telling tales, improvising, playing,
and we are all that Spirit, our stories all
but one cosmic story that we are love indeed,
that perfect love in me seeks the love in you,
and if our eyes could ever meet without fear
we would recognize each other and rejoice
for love is life believing in itself.

O Humankind, we must stop fearing life,
fearing each other, we must absolutely
stop hating ourselves, resenting Creation . . . Life,
O Humankind, life is the only treasure.
We are the custodians of it, it is our sacred trust.
Life is wondrous, awesome and holy, a burning glory,
and its price is simply this: Courage . . .
we must be brave enough to love.

Hear my heart's prayer, O Humankind,
trust in love, don't be afraid. I love you
as I love life, I love myself, please
love me too, love yourself, for perfect love,
as a wise one said, casts out all fear.
If we are to live there is no other choice,
for love is life believing in itself.

                    Above all,
let us set the children free, break the traps
of fear that history has fashioned for them,
free to grow, to seek and question, to dance and sing,
to be dreamers of tomorrow's Rainbows,
and if we but give them our trust
they will guide us to a New Creation,
for love is life believing in itself.

Hear, O Humankind, the prayer of my heart.

                              — *Manitonquat*

Glossary

Acushnet (Uk <u>oosh</u> net) — one of the old bands of the mainland Wampanoag.

Ahtookis (Ah <u>took</u> is) — The Wolf.

Anawon (<u>An</u> uh won) — an elder counselor to Metacomet.

Aquinnah (Ak <u>win</u> uh) — The Bright Cliffs. 2. one of the five bands of the Wampanoag remaining today.

Assonet (Uh <u>sonn</u> et) — one of the five bands of the Wampanoag remaining today.

Assawompsetts (As sa <u>womp</u> set) — one of the old bands of the Wampanoag.

Awashonks — a woman chief of the Wampanoag in the 17th century.

Capowack — one of the old bands of the Wampanoag on Nope (Martha's Vineyard).

Chappaquiddick (Chap pa <u>quid</u> dick) — one of the old bands of the Wampanoag on Nope (Martha's Vineyard).

Checksuwand (<u>Check</u> su wand) — Spirit of the West.

Cheepii (<u>Cheep</u> ee ee) — a mischievious character in Wampanoag legend.

Cohannet — one of the old bands of the mainland Wampanoag.

Deganawida (Day gahn ah <u>weed</u> uh) — a Huron prophet, the giver of the Great Law of Peace.

Epanow (<u>Ee</u> puh no) — a sachem of Aquinnah.

Glooscap (<u>Gloos</u> cap) — a Hero–Deity of the Wabanaki.

Granny Squannit (<u>Skwaw</u> nit) — a character in Wampanoag folktales.

Hobomoko (Hob o <u>muck</u> o) — a character in the Wampanoag Creation stories.

Houdenousonie (Hoo den o <u>so</u> nee) — the people of the longhouse (Iroquois).

185

K'tahdin (Kay <u>tah</u> din) — sacred mountain of the Penobscot.

Katama (Kah <u>tam</u> ah) — a daughter of a chief in old tales of Nope.

Keesuckquand (<u>Kee</u> suck quand) —a spirit of the heavens.

Kiehtan (<u>Kee</u> tan) — The Big Spirit, Creator.

Kishtannit (Kish <u>tah</u> nit) — The Big Spirit, Creator.

manitou (<u>mahn</u> ee too) — spirit.

Mashantanpaine (Mah shan <u>tan</u> pay nee) — a sachem of the Nobscussett.

Massasoit (Mass a <u>so</u> it) — great leader.

Matahdou — Hero–Deity of the Wampanoag; twin brother of Maushop.

Mattapoisett (Mat ta <u>poi</u> set) — one of the old bands of the mainland Wampanoag.

Maushap (<u>Mo</u> shop) — principle Hero–Deity of the Wampanoag.

Metacomet (Met ah <u>cohm</u> it) — a great chief, second son of Ousemequin.

Mettanokit (Met tah <u>no</u> kit) — Mother Earth.

Mettaponsett (Met tah <u>pon</u> set) — one of the old bands of the main land Wampanoag.

minatou (<u>min</u> ah too) — a keeper of the lore.

Monadnock (Mon <u>add</u> nock) — "Mountain That Stands Alone."

Montaup — an old band of the Wampanoag.

Nanummy–in — Spirit of the North.

Narragansett (Narr a <u>gan</u> set) — a nation south of the Wampanoag.

Nemasket (Neh <u>mask</u> et) — one of the five bands of the Wampanoag remaining today.

nepaushet (nuh <u>paw</u> shet) — the sun.

Nipmuc — a nation west of the Wampanoag.

Nisqually — A nation of Western Washington.

Nobscusett — one of the old bands of the Wampanoag on Cape Cod.

Noman's Land (<u>No</u> muns) — an island southwest of Nope.

Nope (<u>No</u> pay) — Wampanoag name of the island of Martha's Vineyard.

Nucksuog (<u>Nuck</u> soo og) — the stars.

Ousemequin (Oo suh <u>mee</u> kwin) — "Yellow Feather," a great leader of the Wampanoag in the 17th century.

paneises (Pan <u>ee</u> sis) — advisors, councilors.

Passaconaway (Pass <u>a</u> con a way) — head chief of the Penacook in the 17th century.

Paumpa gussett — Great Water Spirit.

Penacook (<u>Pen</u> a cook) — nation along the Merrimac river.

Penobscot (<u>Peh</u> nob scot) — nation occupying the watershed of the Penobscot river.

pesuponk — sweat lodge.

Pocasset — an old band of the mainland Wampanoag.

Pokonoket (Po ko <u>no</u> ket) — "Land of the Bitter Bays." 2. old mainland Wampanoag Federation.

Potanit — Spirit of the Fire.

sachem (<u>sah</u> chem) — chief.

Sakonnet (Sa <u>kon</u> net) — one of the old bands of the mainland Wampanoag

Scargo (<u>Scar</u> go) — daughter of a Nobscussett chief in Wampanoag folk tales.

Sequanakeeswush (Se kwan uh <u>kees</u> wush) — spring moon ceremonies.

Sowanand (<u>So</u> wa nand) — Spirit of the South.

Sowunishen (So <u>wun</u> ish en) — southwest wind.

Squant — wife of Maushop.

Squawannit (Skwa <u>wan</u> nit) — sprirt of woman.

Tashin — wind spirit.

Titticut — river of the Pokonoket.

Towuttin — south wind.

Wabanaki (Wah ban <u>a h</u> ki) — "People of the Dawn": Mic–mac, Maliseet, Passamaquoddy and Penobscot.

Wachusett (Wa <u>choo</u> set) — a mountain in central Massachusetts.

Wampanand — Spirit of the Morning Light (East).

Wampanoag (Wam pa <u>no</u> og) — People of the Morning Light.

Wamsutta (Wam <u>sut</u> tah) — brother of Metacomet, elder son of Ousemequin.

Weetamoo — woman chief of the Pocassett.

Watuppa — A lake at Fall River.

Weetucks (<u>We</u> tucks) — a Wampanoag prophet.

wuniish (<u>wun</u> ee ish) — go in beauty, may it be beautiful for you.

ABOUT THE AUTHOR

Medicine Story (Manitonquat), is an elder, storyteller, keeper of the lore, and spiritual leader of the Assonet band of the Wampanoag nation. He is a member of the Association for Humanistic Psychology, a co–founder of the Tribal Healing Council, and has long been involved in the North American Indian Spiritual Unity Movement. One of his many roles is the facilitation of healing circles in men's prisons.

An international lecturer and workshop leader, Medicine Story uses storytelling as a force for individual, community and planetary healing. His stories from indigeneous peoples and cultures around the world seek to illuminate common human values and solutions to problems for people of all ages and backgrounds. He frequently travels to Europe where he shares his wisdom and stories.

He is a former writer and poetry editor with the internationally acclaimed journal *Akwesasne Notes*. The author now makes his home in New Hampshire, among an intentional community of people learning to retribalize. His community, Mettanokit, serves as a model for self–sufficient living, and is also a learning experience for people removed from their tribal roots. Mettanokit is also the center for Story Stone Publications and other educational and outreach programs.

For a catalog of storytelling cassettes by Manitonquat and additional publications of Story Stone or information about workshops and lectures write to:

Story Stone Publications
Mettanokit Outreach
Rte 123
Greenville, N.H. 03048

Proceeds from sales and events go towards Manitonquat's expanding programs of counseling for native families, alcohol & drug abuse counseling, and prison programs. Donations may be designated for assisting any of these programs, or for the Indian Spiritual and Cultural Training Council, or the Wampanoag Reservation Improvement Fund.

OTHER BOOKS AVAILABLE THROUGH PUBLISHER

Black Dawn/Bright Day by Sun Bear with Wabun Wind. Many people are writing about how the Earth is being destroyed. *Black Dawn/Bright Day* is written by an Earth–keeper who tells you why. . . and how to survive. It includes information on places to be and avoid, catastrophe and survival preparation, and maps detailing what Spirit has told Sun Bear will occur on each continent. *"One of the great visionaries of our time, Sun Bear, like Edgar Cayce, offers explicit forecasts that can be ignored only at our own peril."* — R. Smith, <u>Venture Inward</u>

The Path of Power by Sun Bear with Wabun Wind and Barry Weinstock. The life story of Sun Bear, medicine teacher of Ojibwa descent. Written in his down–to–earth, humorous style, he shares his background, his visions, and the path he has followed to fulfill them. Through this book, you come to understand the need for the sacred teachings he has dedicated his life to sharing with the rest of the world. Through his words, discover how to follow your *own* Path of Power, and to walk in balance on the Earth Mother.

Self–Reliance Book by Sun Bear, Wabun Wind & Nimimosha. According to ancient prophesies, and the knowledge given by Spirit, Sun Bear knows that we are in a time of major Earth changes. During this time, groups of people are seeking to return to a way of living more in balance with Nature. The authors present the technical skills for self–reliance with an attitude of respect for the Earth. In an engaging and accessible format, this self–reliance manual also weaves stories, poems, prophecy and humor.

Book of the Vision Quest by Steven Foster and Meredith Little. For all those longing for renewal and personal transformation. The authors portray the courage and passion of those who seek vision to give meaning to their lives. The essence of this solitary journey of mind, body and spirit is clearly conveyed by the authors. They intimately examine the steps of severence, threshold and return that make up the ceremony of Vision Quest.

Order From: Bear Tribe Pubishing, PO BOX 9167, SPOKANE WA 99209
Black Dawn/Bright Day is $9.95. The other books are $10.95. Postage is $2.00 for first book and 60¢ each additional. Or send $1.00 for complete catalog.